COMPARATIVE ESSAYS FOR

OCR A2 ENGLISH LITERATURE

Lead author: Julian Thompson
Introduction: David Johnson

Essay contributors:

Martin Garrett

Anna Beer

Catherine Thompson

Peter Doughty

Lynn Robson

Julian Thompson

David Cockburn

Official Publisher Partnership

OXFORD
UNIVERSITY PRESS

Great Clarendon Street, Oxford OX2 6DP

Oxford University Press is a department of the University of Oxford.
It furthers the University's objective of excellence in research,
scholarship, and education by publishing worldwide in

Oxford New York

Auckland Cape Town Dar es Salaam Hong Kong Karachi
Kuala Lumpur Madrid Melbourne Mexico City Nairobi
New Delhi Shanghai Taipei Toronto

With offices in

Argentina Austria Brazil Chile Czech Republic France Greece
Guatemala Hungary Italy Japan South Korea Poland Portugal
Singapore Switzerland Thailand Turkey Ukraine Vietnam

Oxford is a registered trade mark of Oxford University Press in the UK
and in certain other countries

© Oxford University Press 2013

Database right Oxford University Press (maker)

First published 2013

British Library Cataloguing in Publication Data

Data available

ISBN 978-019-839044-2

10 9 8 7 6 5 4 3 2 1

Printed in Great Britain by Bell and Bain Ltd., Glasgow

Contents

Introduction

Unit F663 Section B requires you to compare two pre-1800 texts: one poetry text and one drama text. Texts are chosen from sixteen possible pairings, and you will be asked to write about them in the light of questions that offer general propositions about aspects of human behaviour reflected in literature.

Comparative writing about texts has been a feature of the study of literature at A level for many years, but this paper is unusual in that it asks you to make a comparison across genres and then allows you freedom in text combination and question choice. The paper also complements a coursework unit (F664) which requires you to compare three texts across genres.

The purpose of this book is to explore the possibilities of the paper by showing you what can be done with textual comparison, and to offer some examples of such comparative work. We hope it will spark off ideas, and suggest approaches. One of the great joys of the paper since its beginning has been the range of responses it has provoked: it is not unusual to find candidates adopting original and very productive arguments through thoughtful choice of questions. Each text's individual qualities should help in defining the qualities of the other: each essay should be an exploration.

Critical essays

This book offers a range of essays on a number of paired texts as examples of independent critical writing. The essays show different approaches to the organization of argument, and they also show different approaches to the use of contextual material (Assessment Objective 4). The examination board does not recommend pairs of texts – this is left to the judgement of you and your teacher. The pairings in this volume were chosen by the authors of the individual essays because they were productive in relation to their chosen topic.

The essays are in no sense 'model essays': they are explorations of possibilities and ideas. It is perhaps just as useful to look at the ways in which each author has chosen to structure his/her comparison, or to approach a particular context, as it is to look at the arguments they are constructing. You should not attempt to 'learn' sections of these essays, or to learn sections of your own draft essays. To come to your examination with fixed views, or a resolve to write about a previously chosen topic, is to constrain the freshness and vitality of your argument.

Sample answers and practice questions

Following the collection of critical essays, this book also includes two candidate-style answers, one of which is representative of an upper-band response and one of which is representative of a middle-band response. It is worth looking at the ways in which these two essays handle their contrasting texts, how the texts are compared and how these comparisons are blended into each argument. We have added examiner-style comments to help you see how a final judgement is reached.

We hope this book helps you to see the possibilities of Unit F663 Section B: to explore new ways of making comparisons and constructing an argument. It is particularly useful to get into the habit of writing questions of your own – to ask yourself 'what would I like to be asked?' A selection of practice questions is included at the very end of this book. A guide to writing questions for F663 Section B can be found among support materials on the OCR website.

Format of assessment

On the OCR two-year Advanced Level literature course, a written paper and a coursework component are offered at each level.

The Assessment Objectives are as follows:

AO1: Articulate creative, informed and relevant responses to literary texts, using appropriate terminology and concepts, and coherent, accurate written expression

AO2: Demonstrate detailed critical understanding in analysing the ways in which structure, form and language shape meanings in literary texts

AO3: Explore connections and comparisons between different literary texts, informed by interpretations of other readers

AO4: Demonstrate understanding of the significance and influence of the contexts in which literary texts are written and received

Course structure

The whole OCR Advanced Level course is made up as follows:

AS Level

Written paper: **F661** *Poetry and Prose 1800–1945* (2 hours)
Section A: Critical analysis of a set poetry text 1800–1945
Section B: Analytical essay on a set prose text 1800–1945

Coursework: **F662** *Literature Post-1900*
Close critical analysis or re-creative writing based on a post-1900 text
An essay exploring connections between **two** texts
At least one text studied for F662 must have been first published or performed after 1990.

The AS course is supported by a recommended critical reading list.

A2 Level

Written paper: **F663** *Drama and Poetry Pre-1800* (2 hours)
Paper F663 is the examined component of the A2 Level literature course: it is a two-section paper. Each section is an hour in length.

Section A: Shakespeare

This section offers a choice of two essay questions on each of four set Shakespeare plays.

You must choose one question, and answer it by presenting a sustained judgement in response to the question's proposition.

The dominant Assessment Objectives for this part of the paper are:

AO2: Demonstrate detailed critical understanding in analysing the ways in which structure, form and language shape meanings in literary texts

AO3: Explore interpretations of other readers

Section B: Drama and poetry pre-1800

This section offers a choice of six generic questions. Candidates must choose one question, and answer it by comparing any one of the four prescribed poetry texts with any one of the drama texts.

The dominant Assessment Objectives for this part of the paper are:

AO3: Explore connections and comparisons between different literary texts, informed by interpretations of other readers

AO4: Demonstrate understanding of the significance and influence of the contexts in which literary texts are written and received

Coursework: **F664** *Texts in Time*
A study of texts across at least two genres within the same or different time period: an essay exploring connections and comparisons between **three** related texts

How to use this book to prepare for F663 Section B

The essays in this collection will support study for F663 Section B by showing some of the ways in which the dominant Assessment Objectives can be fulfilled.

AO3 is fulfilled by showing connections and comparisons between both texts, and by demonstrating awareness of different critical views.

AO4 is fulfilled by exploring some of the contextual influences, which can be found in both texts: these include social or historical contexts; literary contexts (considering contemporary works of literature or other works in the same genre); biographical contexts; a consideration of the critical reception of a text over time; or in the case of a play, the performance history.

Deceit and Self-Deception in *The Wife of Bath's Prologue and Tale* by Geoffrey Chaucer and Ben Jonson's *Volpone*

Martin Garrett

'Men were deceivers ever,' warns a song in *Much Ado About Nothing*, and literature is full of deceiving men and of deceiving women, people in disguise and people who can, as Hamlet puts it, 'smile, and smile, and be a villain', compulsive liars, practical jokers. It is not difficult to find examples of deceit in *The Wife of Bath's Prologue and Tale* (written about 1387–1400) or *Volpone* (1605–6).

The Wife's husbands and Volpone's would-be heirs are duped or falsely persuaded. Volpone plays the parts of an expiring invalid, Scoto of Mantua, and an officer of the court, while Alisoun acts a wronged or lovesick woman. She invents a dream to help persuade Jankyn 'he hadde enchaunted me' (line 575), and Mosca invents scenarios to show the legacy-hunters how hard he is working for them. The Wife and Volpone deceive people into thinking they are dead. There is much self-deception too. Sir Politic lives so deep in delusion that Peregrine wonders 'Does he gull me, trow? Or is gulled?' (Act 2, Scene 1, line 24). It simply does not occur to Volpone, concentrating on his own pleasures, seeking new ways to 'cocker up my genius' (Act 1, Scene 1, line 71), that Mosca will betray him. The Knight in the Wife's tale, having as yet apparently learned nothing since he raped a young woman, thinks that if he can simply produce the right answer to the queen's question 'What thyng is it that wommen moost desiren' (line 905) he will at once be released from the consequences of his crime. On the other hand some people feel that the happy ending of the tale is mere wish-fulfilment on the part of the narrator – the dream of an Alisoun who is, as Helen Cooper provocatively puts it, 'an incurable romantic, a secret Mills and Boon[1] addict'.

Some moralists in both the fourteenth and the seventeenth century would have said that all deception is simply wrong. The biblical injunctions are clear: the devil is the father of lies (John 8:44), and 'Thou shalt not bear false witness' (Exodus 20:16). But in practice some lies seem to be more acceptable than others. Presenting yourself initially as a hag (albeit in a fairy tale) may be a morally useful step if it enables you to educate a rapist knight into a better attitude to women and to 'gentillesse'. In *Volpone* audiences may find themselves debating whether Volpone's and Mosca's comprehensive fraud is justified since it exposes the no less fraudulent nature of such figures as Corbaccio, Corvino and Voltore.

The protagonists of most of Jonson's comedies similarly expose deceivers worse than themselves, but remain unpunished. A good example is Face in

---

1   Mills and Boon, prolific publishers of romantic fiction.

The Alchemist (1610). On the other hand Volpone's use of disguise to attempt to rape Celia is certainly beyond the pale. One factor that complicates such judgements is that literature and drama are inherently deceptive: they involve fiction, telling tales, acting roles, rather than simple truth. How far does our love of a story well told, of an actor's or a character's theatrical verve, blind us to the morality or immorality of deceit? A reader may wonder whether to believe anything Alisoun of Bath says – after all, she is very good at falsely accusing her old husbands – but enjoy the zest and the skill with which she constructs the lies and her own narrative presence. Possibly Chaucer's awareness of the danger of such immersion in the many deceptions of *The Canterbury Tales* is reflected in the final 'retraction'[2] in which he renounces all his secular poems as 'worldly vanitees', including those tales likely to lead towards sin. But Jonson seems more particularly worried by such dangers, partly because the deceptions in *Volpone* are more obviously harmful than the Wife's. Accordingly he deals out punishment to his rogues at the end of the play in an avowed attempt to tackle the Puritan accusation, referred to in his prefatory Epistle, that 'we never punish vice in our interludes'. On the other hand he makes Volpone and Mosca so inventive in wit and intrigue that their harsh fate may seem, as Jonson admits, to violate 'the strict rigour of comic law' – the spirit of comedy itself.

The fact that deceit in *Volpone* is punished more sharply than in *The Wife of Bath's Prologue and Tale* is partly a matter of genre: Jonson is writing satirical comedy with an avowed didactic aim – more than 'a little salt remaineth', as he puts it in the prologue, with which to sting the deceitful times. And drama more generally must score points rapidly as the action on stage moves continually forwards. A monologue like the Wife's works more cumulatively to expose the speaker. Her repeated variations on 'thou seyest', for instance, remind the reader, in conjunction with the fact that Alisoun herself speaks for so long and so volubly, that she is putting words in the mouths of the old men – 'And al was fals' (line 382), as she eventually admits. The *Wife of Bath's Tale* does introduce a serious crime but, in the rather leisurely fashion of many romances, is less interested in punishment than in exploring the extent of the perpetrator's self-deception and taking him through a process of re-education at the hands of the hag.

The sharper satire of *Volpone* responds also to some of the particular concerns of Jonson's time. Ostensibly the play is set in the Venetian Republic[3], famed for its commerce, secular values and wealth (Volpone delights in receiving 'bright sequins', Act 1, Scene 4, line 69, and 'Huge,/Massy, and antique' plate, Act 1, Scene 2, lines 92–3).

---

2 Chaucer's 'retraction' comes at the end of the tale told by the devout Parson and has been seen as variously affected by the Parson's views, as Chaucer's genuine death-bed repentance, or as somehow tongue-in-cheek.

3 The republic, which flourished in late medieval and early modern times, is also the setting for Shakespeare's *Othello* and *The Merchant of Venice*.

Travellers and writers took an especial, often prurient interest in the rich, alluring and no doubt deceiving Venetian courtesans. Mosca plays on this obsession: Lady Would-be is willing to see courtesans everywhere – in boats, disguised as Peregrine, in the innocent Celia. But the play has just as much to say about contemporary London as about tourist Venice. To Jacobean moralists it seemed that ruthless new business practices were replacing older, more honourable and truthful ways of dealing. Tricksters, it was feared, were everywhere. King James I, soon after becoming King of England in 1603, effectively sold knighthoods to anyone who could afford them; we can imagine the aspiring ('Would-be') Sir Pol as one such nouveau knight. The new court was full of faction and intrigue, most famously the Gunpowder Plot of 1605, of which Jonson seems to have had some surprisingly close experience. He was himself a Catholic at the time of this narrowly prevented Catholic-led plot to blow up king and Parliament. (He reconverted to the Church of England in 1610 or later.) Ian Donaldson, Jonson's most recent biographer, speculates that he may have been 'an accomplice or adviser to the conspirators, a neutral observer at their discussions, or (more likely) an agent planted by Sir Robert Cecil to flush out the conspiracy'. Certainly he was employed by the government in the immediate aftermath of the Gunpowder discovery. The plots and counter-plots of *Volpone*, then, may have had particular contemporary resonance, somewhat accounting even for Sir Pol's passion for conspiracy theories. It seems a little unlikely, however, that the Spaniards hired a whale to 'subvert' an English fleet or that Stone the fool received messages in cabbages or sent them in toothpicks.

In Jacobean society leaders were not always what they appeared; gentlemen could be potential Gunpowder assassins, knights could be more 'would-be' than 'politic', just as the magnifico Volpone turns out to be a con-man. One can link this with the discussion of 'gentillesse' in *The Wife of Bath's Tale*, where the old woman lucidly reminds the knight that we are deceiving ourselves if we think 'gentil' blood guarantees the virtuous behaviour for which the ancestors were originally called 'gentil'. The knight had presumed on his rank both in the casualness of his original crime and in his dismissal of his new wife as one 'comen of so lough (low-born) a kynde'(line 1101). Social rank and the obligations that went with it were a matter of some sensitivity in the late fourteenth century, especially in the wake of the Peasants' Revolt of 1381, with its radical rhyme 'When Adam delved and Eve span,/Who was then the gentleman?'. Chaucer, a civil servant with close contacts with the court of Edward III and his successor Richard II, certainly did not support such challenges to the existing social hierarchy. Nevertheless it seems appropriate that the work of a man professionally involved with people of a range of social backgrounds, himself close to power but not a nobleman, registers the danger of assuming a necessary correlation between rank and virtue.

Jonson, although his origins were humbler – his stepfather was a bricklayer, Chaucer's father a prosperous vintner – also came into close contact with members of the nobility and gentry, mainly as patrons of his writing. (An early, unknown patron paid for his education at Westminster School, the foundation of his considerable classical learning.) He was, necessarily, good at flattering great ones – enough, probably, to get him out of jail when the co-authored play *Eastward Ho!* (1605) unwisely criticized the Scots – but this kind of self-abasement must have rankled sometimes with someone as independent-spirited as Jonson. In 1616 he published his plays with the defiantly literary title *Works*, attempting, with some success, to raise his own status and that of playwrights more generally. At this time the work of playwrights tended to be regarded as ephemeral; mere 'plays'. It is perhaps significant, in view of what he saw as his own self-earned position, that the only characters in *Volpone* who have titles – the aptly named Would-bes – are essentially fake gentlefolk. True gentlemen and gentlewomen are not supposed to be credulous, venal, self-seeking, to bear false witness or to end up being drubbed and humiliated in a tortoise-shell.

The Wife of Bath's social status is also of interest. Research has suggested that there were, in medieval England, independent and successful female clothiers like the Alisoun described in the General Prologue. But it is difficult to judge how far she is presented as confident or 'feisty' or how far, as a woman in a mainly patriarchal society, and someone of lower status than a number of her fellow pilgrims, she is trying to assert her independence by all the means at her disposal: the hat as big as a shield, the red stockings, putting down the Friar, out-talking husbands and pilgrims alike. If so, she is much better at impressing her listeners than the overbearing but too easily hoodwinked and too obviously venal Lady Would-be.

But the main issue readers must face in 'placing' Alisoun, and in deciding how far she can be classed as deceitful or self-deceiving, is the question of her use and abuse of her sources[4]. Misogynists' views are deftly diverted or rendered absurd: Theophrastus's polemic is put in the mouths of the old husbands; Jankyn won't stop reading extracts from his book of 'Valerie and Theofraste' until Alisoun hits him and rips out three pages. She seizes any advantage she can, using the arguments of Jovinian given by his opponent Jerome, and leaving out as much as she puts in: for instance 'the wise kyng, daun Salomon' may have had 'wyves mo than oon' (lines 35–6), but she fails to mention that the wives 'turned away his heart' from God (I Kings 11:4). Some modern commentators, such as D.W. Robertson, believe that informed medieval readers or listeners would have noted such abuse of the learned 'auctoritees', or at least some of them. They would have concluded that the Wife is a typically deceiving daughter of Eve, immediate cause of the Fall of Man in Genesis. Her feminist arguments are plausible only to the ignorant, a proof of

---

4   Useful selections from the source material are provided in V.A. Kolve and Glending Olson, eds, *The Canterbury Tales: Nine Tales and the General Prologue* (1989).

the misogynists' point that women were incapable of book-learning. But for other readers her massaging of the sources is a sign of the sheer skill of Alisoun's and/ or Chaucer's assault on misogyny. She turns the tables, seizes the initiative, and is justified in going to any lengths to survive in a patriarchal society. She relies not on tedious scholarly arguments, but on 'Experience'. She strikes pre-emptively at the old husbands before they can dominate her. Ripping pages from Jankyn's book is more desperate and risky but indicates clearly the need to stand up to the 'auctoritees', to question the familiar examples. Celia and Bonario – who are also ranged against established authority – do not stand up very vigorously for themselves in court and nearly fall victim to their less morally squeamish adversaries.

'Who peyntede the leon, tel me who?' (line 692) Alisoun might ask readers who see her whole narrative as designed to deceive. The rhetorical question itself (answer: men) is an instance of the irrepressibility readers tend to like in her. Like Volpone and Mosca, and unlike the straightforward, undeceiving Celia and Bonario, she has 'the gift of the gab'. As already noted, there is naturally a sympathetic response to entertainers, players of parts, spinners of tales – a tendency to believe or at least enjoy Alisoun's bravura account of her life, to revel in Volpone's performances and Mosca's plots and to scorn the more dull and amateur efforts of their dupes. But such reactions must survive a difficult test when an example of theatrical display by Volpone leads to the near-rape of Celia. Here we see him at his most self-deluding. His seduction method is completely misguided. To Celia, who values honesty and loyalty, he offers concealment. He offers Protean change and disguise when she wants stability: dressing up for sex-games as a 'Brave Tuscan lady', a courtesan, or a 'cold Russian' (Act 3, Scene 7, lines 227–31) can have no appeal for her. The falseness of what he offers her is further underlined by its derivativeness: much of his seduction song adapts a well-known poem by Catullus[5], and the 'changèd shapes' (line 220) that he suggests they try out originate in Ovid's *Metamorphoses*[6].

Volpone, like the knight when he raped the maiden 'maugree hir heed' (line 887), will not listen to Celia's pleas; he wants not her but his self-gratifying, self-deluding version of her, the presumptuous 'my Celia' of his song. He wants to change costumes, but cannot change himself: he was already playing parts as a young man when 'For entertainment of the great Valois,/I acted young Antinous'. The aim was already to attract 'The eyes and ears of all the ladies present' rather than to relate to them on a less superficial level (Act 3, Scene 7, lines 161–3). The Valois reference places this 'entertainment' thirty-odd years before the play was composed, in 1574, when

---

5   Gaius Valerius Catullus (c. 84 BCE – c. 54 BCE) poet of the late Roman Republic, has a reputation for heterosexual and homosexual erotic verse. The poem Volpone alludes to (*Carmina* V) is a famous example in the *carpe diem* or 'seize the day' tradition.

6   Publius Ovidius Naso (43 BCE – c. 18 CE), whose work dates from the time of the Emperor Augustus, has, like Catullus, a reputation for raunchy or decadent writing.

Henri III of France was given a famously lavish welcome by Venice. Does that mean that now, in 1605 or 1606, old Volpone cuts an absurd figure? In some productions he is visibly half-disguised still as a bedridden invalid, bedclothes hanging off him, his face greased. (The Wife of Bath seems to have learned more from her boasted 'Experience'.) Volpone tries to ape his youthful performance. Perhaps his singing voice is cracked, perhaps he attempts youthful dance-movements and fails comically. But at the climax of the scene, when he throws aside all pretence and cries 'Yield, or I'll force thee' (line 265), any laughter will probably stop. Most audiences find it difficult not to sympathize here with the vulnerable, frightened Celia, even if elsewhere in the play, many people feel she is a rather insipid figure.

Perhaps, then, *Volpone* is a forthright condemnation of deceit and self-deception, a play whose animal fable well sums up its characters: the sly fox acting according to type as do the vulture, crow, or flesh-fly. For commentators such as D.W. Robertson the Wife stands similarly condemned for her use of knowing deception, while remaining dangerously attractive like Milton's Satan in *Paradise Lost*. But audiences do not usually dismiss 'limber' Mosca (Act 3, Scene 1, line 7) and wily Volpone as villains only. After Bonario intervenes to save Celia, Volpone feels 'unmasked, unspirited, undone' (Act 3, Scene 7, line 277): but it is just a brief moment of stage time, and then the action moves on. Thanks to Mosca's quick thinking a new deception is soon under way and Volpone recovers his nerve. Away from the horror of the attempted rape itself, characters and audience are immersed in the plot to conceal it; with Volpone offstage for most of Act 4 the focus is on Mosca's orchestration of the outrageous lies which Corbaccio, Corvino, Voltore and Lady Would-be are only too happy to tell or endorse if riches may result. In Act 5 some actors of the role stress how self-deluded Volpone is in his final overreaching, but it is equally possible that audiences will enjoy this last flourish of theatricality.

Volpone's and Mosca's deceit climaxes in an absurd double-act, as master-as-servant and parasite-as-master exchange desperate asides. Volpone eventually throws off his disguise, but his closing line 'This is called mortifying of a Fox' (Act 5, Scene 12, line 125) sounds less like a solemn admission of due punishment than a wry admission that the game is up, the hunt – and the show – over. Already the actor seems to be stepping outside his role; he refers to himself in the third person and reminds us of his place in the animal fable or the title of the play. A minute or two later he will return to speak the epilogue, appealing directly to the audience for judgement and – so soon after the Avvocati have passed sentence on him – applause. It feels as if the old trickster has once more escaped. As the edges blur between fictive and actual performer, judgement becomes more difficult. In admitting that he is an actor he vindicates, it may be argued, his earlier deceptions and impersonations.

To foreground thus the conventions of comedy is to admit, to some extent, that the audience, not just some doddery Corbaccio, have been deceived by what happens on stage. The fictive nature of *The Wife of Bath's Prologue and Tale* is also made clear. That the Wife is as much a compendium of sources as a character – she often quotes the *Roman de la Rose*[7] directly, for instance – may remind us that her view is presented as one among many and is part of a larger debate. For a while we have probably been deceived into taking Alisoun at her own valuation, but within the larger structure of *The Canterbury Tales* her ideas on women and marriage are set against those of other pilgrims such as the Merchant and the Franklin, her robust self-presentation contrasted with meeker female pilgrims and characters, such as the Prioress, or Dorigen in *The Franklin's Tale*, or Griselda in *The Clerk's Tale*. Her romance is only one kind of story, one way of seeing, along with bawdy *fabliaux*, sermons, tales of noble suffering and parodies.

In some readings the illusion of one coherent Alisoun is punctured, and the layering of her prologue and tale in the context of *The Canterbury Tales* as a whole becomes apparent: the presence of other pilgrims, of 'Chaucer the pilgrim' as narrator, and behind him perhaps 'Chaucer the poet'. The Friar-bashing early in the Wife's tale sounds like vintage Alisoun, retaliating for the Friar's 'This is a long preamble of a tale!' (line 831). But even here contemporaries may have been less aware of character and more of the wider context of an attack on friars in the reformist views of the Lollards[8]. Within the same tale, the hag's carefully reasoned sermon on 'gentillesse' sounds much less like the Alisoun of the prologue. As elsewhere in *The Canterbury Tales*, the closeness of the relation between teller and tale is loose and variable.

At the end of the tale, arguably, we move back through all of Chaucer's narrative layers. A romantic conclusion gives way to the much more Wife-like prayer to be sent 'Housbondes meeke, yonge, and fressh abedde' and be rid of those who won't be 'governed by hir wyves' (lines 1259, 1262) and won't spend on them. Next we move out, with the Wife still briefly present, to *The Friar's Prologue*. The Friar raises the possibility of further debate on the matter of her tale, but soon proceeds towards his own tale and his own anti-Summoner agenda. The Host, as master of ceremonies, intervenes – his presence in itself a reminder of the larger narrative structure – and the new tale, very unlike Alisoun's, gets under way. The effect of this movement outwards can be rather giddying: the dominant figure of the Wife recedes swiftly from view. Were we deceived into taking this larger-than-life figure for real? Did she, as perhaps Mosca and Volpone did at the beginning of the play, deceive us into thinking hers the only available perspective? 'The insistent relativity of the structuring of the *Canterbury Tales*', says Helen Cooper, who might equally

---

7   The *Roman de la Rose* or 'The story of the Rose' is an allegorical poem composed in France by Guillaume de Lorris and Jean de Meun in the thirteenth century. The allegorical poem focuses on chivalry and courtly love.

8   Lollards were followers of John Wyclif (c. 1320–84) who sought radical reform of the Church.

have been thinking of the 'labyrinth' of meaning in *Volpone*, 'serves to undermine the notion of literature as a vehicle for some fixed and accessible truth'.

Further reading
Jonson
Anne Barton, *Ben Jonson: Dramatist* (1984)
Richard Allen Cave, *Ben Jonson* (1991)
Ian Donaldson, *Ben Jonson: A Life* (2011)
Brian Parker and David Bevington, eds. *Volpone* (1999)
Richard Willmott, ed., *Ben Jonson: Volpone*, Oxford Student Texts edition (2012)

Chaucer
Larry D. Benson, ed., *The Riverside Chaucer* (1988)
Helen Cooper, *Oxford Guides to Chaucer: The Canterbury Tales* (1996)
Steven Croft, ed., *Geoffrey Chaucer: The Wife of Bath's Tale*, Oxford Student Texts edition (2007)
V.A. Kolve and Glending Olson, eds, *The Canterbury Tales: Nine Tales and the General Prologue* (1989)
Jill Mann, *Feminizing Chaucer* (2002)
Derek Pearsall, *The Life of Geoffrey Chaucer* (1992)
D.W. Robertson, *A Preface to Chaucer* (1962)

Attitudes to Self in Ben Jonson's *Volpone* and *Paradise Lost* Book IX by John Milton

Anna Beer

Volpone, 1605, and *Paradise Lost*, 1667, were both written in the seventeenth century, and are therefore imbued with some of the debates about the self that occurred in that century. It can be helpful to consider the literary works in light of these debates, particularly where they are unfamiliar to us now[1]. Here, I will discuss two questions important to the contemporaries of Jonson and Milton, and try to show their relevance to *Volpone* and *Paradise Lost* Book IX: what was the nature of the self? And what would happen to society if the individual became more important?

The first question was usually answered in Christian terms. Particularly relevant to *Volpone* and *Paradise Lost* was the perceived struggle, within the self, between reason and appetite. Man, created by God in his image, had been given reason to control the base desires or appetites of the body. Female ability to reason was seen as weaker than male, a belief that justified men's superior position in society, just as the presence of reason in humanity justified its control over animals. It is in terms of an ongoing battle between reason and appetite that seventeenth-century writers often explored what we might today call psychological struggles between different aspects of the self.

The second question created much anxiety, with commentators seeing an excessive focus on the individual as a challenge to traditional ideals of community. If it was every man for himself, then what happens to society? Two aspects of this concern are particularly relevant to the structure and themes of *Volpone* and *Paradise Lost*. During this period, writers began to produce a new kind of literature, in which they looked inward, exploring their inner selves. Shakespeare led the way in his *Sonnets*, and plays such as *Hamlet*[2]. One question we might ask, therefore, is to what extent Jonson and Milton demonstrate this new concern with inwardness. Secondly, seventeenth-century society had clear rules as to how individuals could and should behave, depending on one's status in society, including strict laws about dress. These days we are now comfortable with, indeed celebrate, the self-made man, or the rags to riches story, or the person who re-makes himself or herself in some way. Attitudes were somewhat different in the seventeenth century. In the light of this, it is fitting that in Shakespeare's comedy *Twelfth Night* (1601), the character Viola,

---

1   Views of the early modern 'self' have been much discussed over the past 25 years. The seminal study is perhaps Stephen Greenblatt's *Renaissance Self-Fashioning* (1980).

2   Shakespeare gives his character Hamlet a highly complex inner life, most evident in his soliloquies, such as the famous 'To be or not to be' *(Hamlet,* c. 1601). He also explores the individual psyche over the course of his 154 *Sonnets* (published 1609).

who is disguised as a boy, says: 'Disguise, I see thou art a wickedness,/Wherein the pregnant enemy does much' (Act 2, Scene 2, lines 26–7).

By calling disguise wicked, she is articulating a common fear. The disguised Viola is distorting her true self. In doing so, she allows the 'enemy' (perhaps the devil) to do his work more easily[3]. It is no coincidence that the devil was seen as the best of actors. Indeed, Satan in *Paradise Lost* is portrayed as such: he 'New part puts on, and as to passion moved' (line 667) works his evil. The use and abuse of disguise, the hiding of the true self, often for evil purposes, is one of the things that link *Volpone* and *Paradise Lost* Book IX, both structurally and thematically. The two authors, however, use disguise, and its inversion, unmasking, in different ways.

In *Volpone*, disguise provides much of the humour. We laugh at Volpone's consummate ability to deceive his aspiring heirs through faking illness. Indeed, our knowing laughter makes us uncomfortably complicit with the villain. This is comedy, however, and we expect the disguises to be penetrated and exposed. Discovering, literally and metaphorically, often lies at the heart of comic plots and usually provides the moral resolution. Volpone's acting ability may be entertaining, but we expect his 'real' self to be revealed and punished by the end of the play.

One example of physical 'discovering' does in fact occur, but to the unfortunate Sir Politic Would-be, who receives his final humiliation while failing to disguise himself as a tortoise. As the stage direction says: 'They pull off the shell and discover him' (Act 5, Scene 4, line 73). When it comes to the exposure of Volpone, however, the play is structured in a complex and thought-provoking way. Midway through *Volpone*, Jonson appears to give the audience what we expect. Celia, on the point of being raped by Volpone, is saved by the hidden Bonario, who witnesses and denounces the Fox. Volpone himself thinks the game is up: 'Oh!/I am unmasked, unspirited, undone,/Betrayed to beggary, to infamy' (Act 3, Scene 7, lines 276–8). Volpone has been wearing various masks, and now his true self is revealed.

However, Jonson does not make the exposure of Volpone's evil so easy. Throughout the following legal process, demands for 'proofs' are ignored, and the words and values of Celia and Bonario, their appeals to conscience, and 'heaven, that never fails the innocent', are dismissed. As the lawyer says, 'These are no testimonies' (Act 4, Scene 6, lines 17–18). Volpone may have been briefly 'unmasked' but he has not been 'undone'.

Is it any different by the end of the play? There are two ways of answering that question, connected to the two endings, that of the dramatic action, and that of the entire entertainment. In the chaotic climax, Volpone throws off his disguise: 'The Fox shall here uncase' (Act 5, Scene 12, line 85). By insisting that he is 'By blood and rank a gentleman' (line 117) of Venice, he hopes to escape the vicious physical punishment

---

3 'Pregnant' here means resourceful, always ready to take advantage.

handed out to Mosca, for impersonating someone of a higher social class. He fails: 'imposture' and 'feigning' are Volpone's crimes, and he is punished accordingly.

> And since the most was gotten by imposture,
> By feigning lame, gout, palsy, and such diseases,
> Thou art to lie in prison cramped with irons,
> Till thou be'st sick and lame indeed. Remove him.
> (lines 121–4)

The Fox is, at last, 'undone'. His punishment is both extreme and fitting. Jonson felt the need to defend the severity of the punishments, which he recognized were at odds with the 'laws' of comedy, but insisted that they were vital in order to get across his moral message[4].

There is, however, one more twist to the play. Having been removed from the stage for punishment, Volpone returns to deliver an epilogue, asking for our applause. Perhaps this is Jonson's wittiest and most profound challenge to his audience. If we applaud the actor who plays Volpone, are we applauding his disguise, the Fox? And, if we are, what does that tell us about ourselves? By raising these questions, *Volpone* demonstrates literature's capacity 'to question, defamiliarize and even transform the sense of who or what we are'[5].

Disguise, of course, is central to the success of Satan's temptation of Eve. However, Milton's villain is neither unmasked nor discovered, at least in Book IX. The reader has to wait until Book X for that to happen[6]. Instead, the most important moment of discovery in Book IX occurs when Adam and Eve realize the enormity of their actions in eating the apple. Milton describes the worst possible morning-after feeling, when Adam and Eve, no longer innocent, 'each the other viewing' with something approaching horror are 'naked left/To guilty shame he covered, but his robe/Uncovered more' (lines 1052, 1057–9). Adam makes coverings, whether actual (a blush?) or merely virtual (out of shame), as 'if to hide/Their guilt and dreaded shame; O how unlike/To that first naked glory!' (lines 1113–5).

That all-important 'if' suggests the impossibility of hiding from God. Paradoxically, Adam and Eve are at the same time clothed ('covered') and

---

4   Jonson defends himself from various attacks in his long Epistle to *Volpone*. With regard to the ending of the play (what he calls its 'catastrophe') he writes: 'And though my catastrophe may, in the strict rigour of comic law, meet with censure, it was done of industry' (i.e. deliberately).

5   This quotation is taken from a chapter called 'Me' which offers a challenging discussion of the representation of the self in literature. See *An Introduction to Literature, Criticism and Theory*, Andrew Bennett and Nicholas Royle (2009).

6   At the very moment that Satan is giving his victory speech, he and all his followers are 'transformed' (Book X, line 519) into serpents. Driven by hunger and thirst, they rush to eat but 'instead of fruit/ Chewed bitter ashes' (lines 565–6). The punishment of Satan and his followers does not end there. Reading this section of Book X reveals much about Milton's understanding of divine justice.

'uncovered'. This is, of course, just *before* they don their fig-leaves. But the true self is always visible to God.

As well as deploying disguise and discovery in different ways, Jonson and Milton can also be compared for the ways in which they depict inwardness. You will have noticed that Jonson's characters (unlike many created by his contemporary, Shakespeare) do not constantly articulate their motives or express their thoughts. They are not given what some critics call 'interiority'. But does this weaken the play *Volpone*? If Jonson's main concern is the fast-paced interplay between characters as types, then why do we need to know about the characters' interior lives?

In any case, though Jonson may concentrate on 'type' and disguise, he does hint at Volpone's inner life. He likes being special ('No common way' for him, Act 1, Scene 1, line 33) and is excited more by the acquisition of wealth than by its possession ('I glory/More in the cunning purchase of my wealth/Than in the glad possession', lines 30–32). Acting is what Volpone lives for, so it is psychologically fitting that even Volpone's erotic fantasies involve role-playing. He envisions Celia as playing the part of a courtesan, or

> some quick Negro, or cold Russian;
> And I will meet thee in as many shapes:
> Where we may so transfuse our wand'ring souls,
> Out at our lips, and score up sums of pleasures
> (Act 3, Scene 7, lines 231–4)

Volpone is as greedy for 'many shapes' as his suitors are for money. Is it possible to understand why he is like this? Jonson does show us a fearful Volpone, drinking to 'fright/This humour from my heart', a man who seeks

> Any device, now, of rare, ingenious knavery,
> That would possess me with a violent laughter,
> Would make me up again!
> (Act 5, Scene 1, lines 11–16)

These glimpses of a Volpone in thrall to his 'humour', acting and drinking to mask his emptiness, perhaps induce understanding of him, maybe even sympathy for him. Both these potential responses to Volpone could well undermine Jonson's stated moral purpose for his drama. This purpose is expressed, convolutedly, in the Epistle to *Volpone*. It is easier to understand in a phrase from another Jonson play, the prologue to *The Alchemist* (1610). Jonson wants 'to better men', or as we would put it, to improve people morally. If Jonson gives Volpone an interior life, and therefore encourages the audience to view him more sympathetically, perhaps even to excuse his deceptions and violations, then the playwright's moral purpose is at best complicated, at worst undermined.

For one critic, however, Jonson achieves his moral purpose by reaching through Volpone's mask to the inner man. The effect is to 'induce a sympathetic understanding of villainy without sentimentalizing the villains'[7].

The same critic argues that Milton accomplishes the same feat in his portrayal of Satan. Milton certainly gives his villain a complex inner life, but he also uses the narrator to guide the reader's response to Satan, a technique unavailable to Jonson in his drama. Milton demonstrates vividly Satan's 'inward grief', his 'bursting passion' (lines 97–8). We hear his eloquent, if self-pitying, expressions of longing when he sees the beauty of Eden ('With what delight could I have walked thee round,/If I could joy in aught', lines 114–5) and learn of his sense of isolation and alienation: 'but I in none of these/Find place or refuge' (lines 118–9). Satan is extremely good at articulating his emotions, suggesting a complex, tortured self-awareness.

Milton's narrator, however, offers a slightly different perspective, nudging the reader towards a less seductive, and more reductive, view of Satan's identity. When Satan sees Eve, her beauty has a remarkable effect upon him; it

> with rapine sweet bereaved
> His fierceness of the fierce intent it brought:
> That space the evil one abstracted stood
> From his own evil
> (lines 461–4)

Without 'his own evil', Satan is 'Stupidly good' (line 465). To regain the power of action, Satan must fill himself once again with evil: 'Fierce hate he recollects, and all his thoughts/Of mischief, gratulating, thus excites' (lines 471–2).

Satan is evil, in the same way that Volpone is the Fox. When Satan is re-introduced in Book IX, Milton subtly steers us towards an understanding of Satan's true self. Satan is described as 'fearless', but we are also told by the narrator that earlier in the poem he 'fled before the threats/Of Gabriel' and 'By night he fled' (lines 53–8). How can he be both fearless, yet on the run? Because it is his actions that show the truth, not deceptive descriptions of action. Satan is only 'fearless' in his own mind. Milton also uses the overall structure of *Paradise Lost*, with its multiple parallels, to prompt a more negative assessment of Satan. For example, in Book IX Satan is unwilling to mix with 'bestial slime'. He does not wish to 'incarnate' his essence (lines 165–6) because his sense of self is a selfish, exclusive one. In contrast, the poem as a whole reveals the Son of God as willing to accept incarnation, willing to transform his divine self into a suffering human self for the sake of humanity[8].

---

7   Gordon Campbell, in his introduction to the Oxford World's Classics edition of *Volpone* in *The Alchemist and Other Plays*, page xiv (1995).

8   The crucial speech comes in Book III, when the Son says: 'on me let thine anger fall;/Account me man; I for his sake will leave/Thy bosom' (lines 237–9). God applauds the Son's decision to 'incarnate'.

For all these narratorial interventions, however, Milton continues to provide insight into Satan's thought processes, revealing his apparent self-awareness ('For only in destroying I find ease/To my relentless thoughts', lines 129–30) and his perverse form of courage:

> Revenge, at first though sweet,
> Bitter ere long back on itself recoils;
> Let it; I reck not
> (lines 171–3)

Satan's eloquent articulations of his inner life are some of the most sophisticated representations of the self in the whole of *Paradise Lost*. This very sophistication may explain why Satan is often seen as the most interesting figure in the poem.

Although the interplay of deception and discovery, and the representation of villains with varying degrees of interiority, link *Volpone* and *Paradise Lost*, it will already be obvious that these two works are preoccupied in different ways with the self.

At first sight, Jonson appears to offer a straightforward understanding of the self. Known as the developer of the 'comedy of humours', Jonson's comic characterization is broadly based on the ancient physiological theory of the four bodily humours. According to this theory, the ideal body is made up of a balance of these four humours, which leads to a well-balanced personality[9]. Jonson, however, creates grotesque individuals operating at the extremes of behaviour. In his dramatic writing it seems that all human beings are ruled by a dominant and often destructive humour. In the Venice of *Volpone*, some characters are driven by egotism; almost all are driven, even possessed, by greed of some kind: 'These possess wealth, as sick men possess fevers,/Which trulier may be said to possess them' (Act 5, Scene 12, lines 101–2).

In his comedy of humours, Jonson is not interested in well-balanced individuals who are capable of change. There is limited scope for a sense of the self as unique or capable of development, if, as Jonson suggests, human beings are possessed by, driven by, a dominant humour. This is already a reductive view of human beings, but Jonson takes the idea even further. In *Volpone*, people are merely beasts. Jonson was writing at a time before animals and nature were viewed in a sentimental way, and so to compare human beings to animals was to demonstrate just how low humans had sunk. Humans are repeatedly referred to as carcasses, and Volpone describes his

---

9   The 'four humours' model for the workings of the human body originated in ancient Greece, and it remained the dominant medical theory in Europe during the seventeenth century. The four humours of blood, phlegm, black bile and yellow bile were linked with the four fundamental elements of air, water, earth and fire.

villainy in terms of cannibalism: 'Why, this is better than rob churches yet;/Or fat, by eating once a month a man' (Act 1, Scene 5, lines 91–2). Volpone has no illusions about human superiority. He repeatedly refers to himself as 'the fox', appearing to relish his bestial identity: 'The fox fares ever best when he is cursed' (Act 5, Scene 3, line 119). Like animals, Jonson's humans are ruled by their appetites. As one critic has pointed out, 'Jonson's world is a jungle of predators and victims, free from the restraint of religion, reason, or respect for tradition'[10]. Religion, reason, and respect for tradition are powerless to control individuals like Volpone and Mosca, partly because they do not believe in any of these things.

Instead, Volpone and Mosca have a very different worldview, which they believe is true for everyone, even those who profess otherwise. Mosca claims that 'All the wise world is little else in nature/But parasites or sub-parasites' (Act 3, Scene 1, lines 12–13).

Mosca's view of 'All' the world echoes Volpone's assertion in the first speech of the play that 'all men' are in thrall to money. This is a simple and brutal view of the self, which for some audiences has at least the virtue of honesty about the human condition. What remains a matter for debate is whether the attitudes of Volpone and Mosca are confirmed by the play as a whole, or whether Jonson, through the tentative glimpse of Volpone's 'self' beneath his disguise, somehow offers an alternative, less reductive, view of the self.

Milton offers a different view. In fact, he offers two competing views of the self, evident in the crisis between Adam and Eve in Book IX. Put simply, Eve wishes to separate temporarily from Adam in order to get more work done in the garden, and she believes that she has the individual strength and ability to withstand the, as yet unknown, 'malicious foe' (line 253). Eve asserts that their happiness in Eden is a frail happiness if they cannot withstand any threat alone, without 'exterior help': 'Eden were no Eden thus exposed' (lines 336, 341). Adam sees things differently, viewing himself and Eve as 'one flesh', mutually dependent, and thus needing to 'mind' each other: 'tender love enjoins,/That I should mind thee oft, and mind thou me' (lines 357–8). His view of the self is underpinned by the theology of *Paradise Lost*. Just as God gave Adam being, Adam gave Eve being. Their identities are therefore linked, with Adam being Eve's creator and protector. As Adam says: Eve should 'leave not the faithful side/That gave thee being, still shades thee and protects'. He goes on to argue that:

> The wife, where danger or dishonour lurks,
> Safest and seemliest by her husband stays,
> Who guards her, or with her the worst endures.
> (lines 265–9)

---

10 Marion Wynne-Davies, ed. *Bloomsbury Guide to English Literature*, page 609 (1989).

Putting aside for the moment the way in which Adam's words establish a gender hierarchy in Eden, the closing phrase here demonstrates that Adam views himself and Eve as an indissoluble unit, for better or for worse. As the critic Nigel Smith notes: 'The relationship between Adam and Eve turns on the meaning of one flesh.' For Adam, he and Eve are not individual selves, but one continuous being. Adam's view is temporarily challenged, but not discarded, when Eve eats the apple. In the highly dramatic section of speech that begins 'How can I live without thee' (line 908), Adam rationalizes his decision to eat the apple too: 'Our state cannot be severed, we are one,/One flesh; to lose thee were to lose my self' (lines 958–9).

Adam clings to this idea even though he is 'not deceived' (line 998). But by insisting that he and Eve remain 'one', the Fall is completed.

Milton challenges us to decide which attitude towards the self is correct. Both are seen to have limitations. Eve's desire for some independence makes her vulnerable to Satan, while Adam's desire for them to be 'one' means he will be unable to resist the fallen Eve. What is clear is that the moment of separation that occurs before the description of the Fall in Book IX, when Eve 'from her husband's hand her hand/ Soft she withdrew' (lines 385–6) is critical. Adam and Eve's hands will not be joined again until the closing lines of the whole poem, when they 'hand in hand' leave Eden. Only then can they even begin to approach Adam's ideal of 'one flesh': two selves as one. Book IX, however, ends with Adam and Eve alienated from each other, from God, and from their own selves, spending the 'fruitless hours' in mutual accusation, 'neither self-condemning' (line 1188).

This is a dismal, hopeless ending, at least if seen in isolation from the rest of Milton's epic. Milton has indeed changed his poem 'to tragic', as he said he would in line 6 of Book IX. Despite *Volpone* being a comedy, and despite the unmasking and punishment of Volpone himself, it is just as hard to take an optimistic view of the human self from Jonson's play as it is from the end of Book IX of *Paradise Lost*. Mosca has earlier spelt out the reason why he and Volpone are so successful in their deceptions of others. Self-absorption (being 'stuffed' with one's 'own hopes') leads to moral blindness in their victims:

> they will not see't.
> Too much light blinds 'em, I think. Each of 'em
> Is so possessed, and stuffed with their own hopes,
> That anything unto the contrary,
> Never so true, or never so apparent,
> Never so palpable, they will resist it –
> (Act 5, Scene 2, lines 22–7)

And Volpone adds 'Like a temptation of the devil'. This is a fine example of Jonson's savage irony. Volpone insists that people will resist truth with the same intensity as they (are supposed to) resist the devil, something that Milton's Eve literally fails to do. Goodness and truth do not stand a chance when we are all 'possessed' and thus blinded by our own selfish desires.

It would be wrong, however, to end a survey of these two powerful works without acknowledging the presence of a different perspective on the self, and one that turns the spotlight upon the inner life, and offers a tentative hope. In Book IX of *Paradise Lost*, Adam articulates what he believes to be the strength and the vulnerability of human beings.

> within himself
> The danger lies, yet lies within his power:
> Against his will he can receive no harm.
> But God left free the will, for what obeys
> Reason, is free, and Reason he made right
> (lines 348–52)

Human beings may struggle with different aspects of their selves, but we have reason and free will to guide and enable us. Milton's work suggests that, if the 'danger' lies within the self, so too does the solution.

Further reading
Critical studies

Anna Baldwin, ed., *John Milton: Paradise Lost Book IX*, Oxford Student Texts edition (2008)

Anna Beer, *John Milton: Poet, Pamphleteer & Patriot* (2008)

Andrew Bennett and Nicholas Royle, *An Introduction to Literature, Criticism and Theory* (2009) – see the chapter 'Me'

Margaret Kean, ed., *John Milton's Paradise Lost: A Sourcebook* (2005)

Matthew Steggle, ed., *Volpone: A Critical Guide* (Continuum Renaissance Drama, 2011)

Richard Willmott, ed., *Ben Jonson: Volpone*, Oxford Student Texts edition (2012)

John Milton's *Paradise Lost* Book IX and John Webster's *The White Devil*: Contrasting Moral Visions of Women

Catherine Thompson

These texts both offer a view of women through a developed portrait of one central female character – Eve in *Paradise Lost* and Vittoria in *The White Devil*. As modern readers, we expect to encounter a female figure who is psychologically persuasive; we understand that she will experience an imagined inner life which is consistent with the way she encounters events and responds to them. However, in Webster's dramatic world there is not necessarily any consistent interior life in his characters; rather, they are driven by external events and by Webster's practice of researching and refining lines of poetry which he later put into their mouths. It is helpful to distinguish the work of Webster and his contemporaries in this respect from Shakespeare. As Simon Trussler says:

> Shakespeare's world is one in which 'character' does indeed begin to take on its modern meaning, of individuals with distinct personalities and a psyche which expresses itself in (or is concealed by) what they do. His contemporaries were perhaps more of their own time in their preference for displaying how action shapes character rather than the reverse (though in thus anticipating the existential sense of selfhood they were arguably no less modern).[1]

Vittoria, then, is a striking figure who meets a set of experiences in an interesting variety of ways; arguably, she scarcely seems to sustain the same character from one of her few scenes to the next. Ultimately, she must be understood to be the sum of her considerably varied parts, and also to take part of her dramatic excitement and energy from the lurid Italian setting in which we find her, much as the Duchess of Malfi, in Webster's other great play, is coloured by what Emma Smith calls 'a kind of voyeuristic tabloid frisson'[2]. As for the moral force of *The White Devil*, Webster never apparently takes an interest in who is to blame for events, or even what has caused them (very unlike Milton in *Paradise Lost* Book IX, as we shall see), but rather is focused on their consequences – the important question is 'what happens next?', and the moral boundaries remain frequently blurred, even, arguably, unexplored by the dramatist. This certainly seems to happen with Vittoria.

Eve, by contrast, is a more consistently psychologized character – the picture of

---

1   Simon Trussler, *Faber Pocket Guide to Elizabethan and Jacobean Drama* (2006)
2   Emma Smith, 'Webster, *The Duchess of Malfi*' Oxford University *Great Writers Inspire* Podcast (2012)

her marriage to Adam seems almost novelistic at times – and is consistently the centre of others' moral judgements. In the later stages of Book IX, the causes and blame for the central event – the Fall of Mankind – is the main preoccupation of the poem. But where Webster seems to work within the constraints of his chosen form, so that character is shaped by the source material, the setting, dramatic convention and the progress of events, Milton has constraints of another kind. His source is of course Genesis[3], and he has expanded and extended the story but cannot alter or contradict it. His stated purpose in the opening lines of *Paradise Lost* – 'to justify the ways of God to men' – requires him to be absolutely faithful to his source and its theological implications: Eve's character and her marriage must be depicted as perfect while she remains sinless, and flawed only after the Fall.

Both characters exist within the patriarchal institution of marriage, and it is tempting for modern readers to assume that, as women existing long before the feminist movements, they therefore have few rights and opportunities for self-determination. Early modern texts such as William Gouge's *Of Domesticall Duties* (1622)[4] make it clear, however, that such matters were not necessarily clear cut, and that there might be some room for manoeuvre within the expected structures. For example, he is quoted by Laurie Maguire as endorsing traditional roles (echoing Genesis) in the following passage: 'Nature hath placed an eminencie in the male over the female: so as where they are linked together in one yoake, it is given by nature that he should governe, she obey.' However, he tempers this view in two other extracts:

> Of all degrees wherein there is any difference betwixt person and person, there is the least disparitie betwixt man and wife.

> If an husband require his wife to doe that which God hath forbidden, she ought not to do it.[5]

It will not do, therefore, to argue that male supremacy was at this time not negotiable. As Maguire's reading of Gouge suggests, our understanding of early modern gender politics depends on which source we read and which bits of it we highlight. In a similar way both Milton and Webster leave latitude as to how their presentations of women should be interpreted.

---

3   For the biblical story of the Fall see Genesis 3:1–24.

4   A popular text of its time discussing the hierarchy of family life. Other such treatises include John Dod and Robert Cleaver's *A Godly form of Household Government* (1598) and William Whately's *A Bride-Bush* (1617).

5   'John Webster', Oxford University Faculty of English, lectures by Emma Smith and Laurie Maguire, Hilary Term 2003.

Vittoria's appearances in the play constitute four contrasting scenes, and each might profitably be juxtaposed with the experiences and behaviour of Eve in *Paradise Lost* Book IX. On Vittoria's first appearance in *The White Devil* (Act 1, Scene 2), she is introduced by her brother Flamineo more or less as a commodity. The play is loosely based on historical events, and it is clear that the historical Vittoria was obliged to marry because of her family's financial plight; her beauty did indeed make her a commodity, and in this scene she is 'trading up' – swapping her lacklustre first husband for a more impressive second. Webster's moralistic sources view Vittoria not just as an adventuress but a hypocrite and whore, and their purpose in retelling the story is to present her as an object entirely deserving of heaven's retribution. Webster, as in his later play *The Duchess of Malfi*, seems less judgemental. In her first scene in *The White Devil*, Vittoria is inscrutable, playing out a love scene with Bracciano in which almost all she says is timidly ambiguous; the cynical ambition that may lie beneath her speeches is voiced not by her, but by her brother Flamineo, who constantly seeks his own advantage and expects preferment from Bracciano in return for the gift of Vittoria.

In case the bargaining element of their relationship might be in any way unclear, Bracciano makes it explicit, saying 'I will but change/My jewel for your jewel' (lines 233–4). From her first appearance in this play, Vittoria is apparently a survivor – watchful, inscrutable, constantly looking for an advantage or an escape route. Her very condition is insecurity. Eve, in contrast, is the very type and model of security: the only woman in existence, adored partner of the only man, and especially favoured by God as the mother of humankind. Where Vittoria looks for a meal ticket, Eve has arguably become – by Book IX – almost stifled by the security and predictability of her situation. Her inferior position in her marriage is firmly established in Book IV:

> though both
> Not equal, as their sex not equal seemed;
> For contemplation he and valour formed,
> For softness she and sweet attractive grace,
> He for God only, she for God in him
> (Book IV, lines 295–9)

Both women are impatient for change, and their desires surface in prophetic dreams. Vittoria's dream of the yew-tree and the grave is darkly violent and Gothic in quality, and sends an ominous message about her own character, either gesturing at Vittoria's moral depravity (in line with the sources) or – perhaps more likely – presenting her as insecure, even unstable: 'Lord, how methought/I trembled, and yet for all this terror/I could not pray' (Act 1, Scene 2, lines 257–9). The dream surely foretells the murders of Isabella and Camillo, but it is Flamineo – always ascribing the worst of motives – who gives voice to the suspicion that Vittoria is issuing implicit commands to Bracciano: 'She hath taught him in a dream/To make away his duchess and her husband' (lines 267–8).

It is for the director – or the audience, or the reader – to decide whether the dream is genuine and mystically prophetic, or whether Vittoria is exploiting a very practical opportunity to make her way. Webster knows the value of such a dream dramatically, and gives a similar, though briefer moment of foresight to the Duchess of Malfi, immediately before she is subject to cruel psychological torture by her brother[6]. The Duchess sees in a dream the diamonds of her coronet changed to pearls, as a warning of tears to come. Eve's account of a dream comes early in Book V of *Paradise Lost*, where it seems that she has divined a threat unclear as yet to Adam[7]. Her dream 'chilled' her with 'damp horror' (line 65), foretelling as it does the scene of her temptation and her fall; it ends with a moment of great excitement when, after tasting the fruit, Eve experiences the power of flight:

> Forthwith up to the clouds
> With him I flew, and underneath beheld
> The earth outstretched immense, a prospect wide
> And various: wondering at my flight and change
> To this high exaltation...
> (Book V, lines 86–90)

Eve's openness to the dream and its accurate foretelling of the temptation to come might suggest a feminine sensitivity, almost a second sight that is withheld from Adam. Its dramatic power is similar to the dreams of Vittoria and the Duchess of Malfi, since it helps to structure the story and move it forward. However, Milton has been scrupulous as always in sustaining the logic of his unfallen world: if Adam and Eve are in Paradise, why is she dreaming of horror and sin? The dream itself has emanated from Satan, who is found by the angels at the end of Book IV 'Squat like a toad, close at the ear of Eve' (line 800); the dream might convince us as a psychological experience of Eve's, but we must also accept that it is authored by the father of lies. This suggestion that Eve's less-than-perfect thoughts may be planted by Satan is very different from Webster's presentation of Vittoria in Act 1, where her motives are kept at a distance from the audience, and arguably are not revealed at all.

---

6   *The Duchess of Malfi* Act 3, Scene 5, lines 12–17.

7   See *Paradise Lost* V, 26–94.

Vittoria's second appearance in *The White Devil* is in her arraignment[8], the play's great set piece (Act 3, Scene 2). Here, far from the distant and enigmatic impression she gave in her earlier appearance, she presents herself as energetic, assertive and even humorous. She appears to be the obvious victim of a set-up, and the audience is likely to be quickly won over by her bravery in isolation. Her rejoinders are quick and apt: she insists on being tried in English rather than let her accusers hide behind the obscurity of Latin, and when the lawyer switches to a complex and wordy legalese (using vocabulary such as 'literated', 'diversivolent' and 'extirp', lines 27–31) Vittoria's lively response – 'Why, this is Welsh to Latin' (line 40)[9] – will surely draw a laugh from the audience. Unusually in a play where there seems to be very little direction of the audience's reaction, Webster does put some clues into the mouths of the ambassadors who act as a kind of chorus: the French Ambassador suggests caution, reminding us that 'She hath lived ill'; the English Ambassador provides balance, however, asserting that 'the Cardinal's too bitter' (lines 107–8). Vittoria is surely the moral victor in her own summing up:

> Terrify babes, my lord, with painted devils;
> I am past such needless palsy. For your names
> Of whore and murd'ress they proceed from you,
> As if a man should spit against the wind,
> The filth returns in's face.
> (Act 3, Scene 2, lines 148–52)

Despite her lively defence, Vittoria is 'confin'd/Unto a house of convertites' (lines 264–5), but remains defiant, uttering one of Webster's highly quotable general truths, or 'commonplace thoughts'[10]: 'Through darkness diamonds spread their richest light' (line 295). This strong, even masculine self-presentation seems a long way from the gentleness of Eve, but Milton's own taste for adversarial argument (he was employed as Cromwell's Latin Secretary)[11] emerges in Eve's firmly argued case for a little more space, a little more independence from Adam. The couple's first conversation in Book IX is initiated by Eve; Alastair Fowler notes that 'Eve speaks

---

8   An arraignment is a formal reading of a criminal complaint in the presence of the defendant. Here, Vittoria is accused of adultery and murder.

9   Shakespeare makes extended use of the unintelligibility of Welsh to an English audience in *Henry IV Part 1*, Act 3, Scene 1.

10 So called because they are ready to be copied out into a 'commonplace book'. Early printed texts of Webster's plays often provided them with quotation marks, or printed them in italics.

11 Milton became Cromwell's Secretary for Foreign Tongues in 1649, and was still in post, as 'Latin Secretary', at Charles II's Restoration in 1660. His task was to explain – as an advocate might – the policies of the English Republic to the rest of Europe, often using the universal language, Latin.

first, something she has not previously done'. Her suggestion that they should divide their gardening tasks and separate to complete them more efficiently seems innocent enough, but her language pre-figures a less innocent world after the Fall:

> the work under our labour grows,
> *Luxurious* by restraint; what we by day
> Lop overgrown, or prune, or prop, or bind,
> One night or two with *wanton* growth derides
> Tending to *wild*.
> (lines 208–12, my italics) [12]

The italicized words have perfectly innocent meanings, suggesting merely that the garden is growing, but Fowler points out that 'Nature has a continual tendency to wildness that Eve is perhaps already beginning to experience almost as a moral temptation'. The couple develop their arguments with impressive logic and apparent patience and love, but in his narrative links Milton shows a growing emotional tension and an unmistakeable determination from Eve – 'sweet' as she is – to have her own way:

> To whom the virgin majesty of Eve,
> As one who loves, and some unkindness meets,
> With sweet austere composure thus replied…
> (lines 270–72)

Eve's bid for independence, often admired by feminist readers, is of course a terrible mistake in the terms of the poem, leading directly as it does to the Fall of Mankind. Her behaviour in this part of the poem presents a challenge to Milton's logical presentation of the Fall, because it is hard to see Eve here as entirely innocent and without sin. Her persistence in spite of Adam's better judgement smacks of defiance. After she has eaten, when she debates with herself as to whether to share the power of the fruit with Adam, she is tempted to keep it a secret to 'keep the odds of knowledge in my power', so that she can:

> add what wants
> In female sex, the more to draw his love,
> And render me more equal, and perhaps,
> A thing not undesirable, sometime
> Superior; for inferior who is free?
> (lines 821–25)

---

12 Note that the words 'Luxurious', 'wanton' and 'wild' in this extract have for the 'fallen' reader morally questionable meanings (wanton = sexually depraved) and these jostle with the 'innocent' meanings of Eve.

True freedom for Eve comes in obeying Adam, thereby obeying God; but it is hard not to sympathize with her desire for more than just obedience. As readers, our own possible admiration for Eve arguably emanates from our status as fallen human beings, and is similar to the impulse that leads us to admire or sympathize with Satan in the poem, also a fallen creature. Milton's exploration of the psychological basis of original sin is complex, implicating the male as well as the female reader. Webster, meanwhile, provides a snapshot of Vittoria turning on her enemies. She is feisty, but no more so than any hunted beast. Is she to be condemned as a rebel, or accorded empathy as a victim? Webster gives no view.

Both Eve and Vittoria offer a vision of women presented from a male perspective, and both are seen to be beautiful, alluring, unaccountable and frustrating to deal with at different times by male characters. Vittoria – who so far has seemed inscrutable in her first scene, and lively and dominant in her arraignment – appears in her third as a 'white devil' to Bracciano, who accuses her of infidelity and rejects her. His speech reflects his frustration at his own attraction to Vittoria, which has made him helpless: 'Your beauty! O, ten thousand curses on't./How long have I beheld the devil in crystal?' (Act 4, Scene 2, lines 86–7).

'The devil in crystal', like 'the white devil', might just carry the meaning 'hypocrite'; however, the shining crystal suggests not just falsity hiding behind a semblance of truth, but falsity overlaid with an irresistible attractiveness to the helpless male victim. But Vittoria turns the tables on the duke at great speed, rejecting him in turn:

> I had a limb corrupted to an ulcer,
> But I have cut it off; and now I'll go
> Weeping to heaven on crutches.
> (lines 120–22)

In the space of one speech she brings Bracciano back to her; he begs that she should be 'at peace' with him again despite what the world might say (line 172). Vittoria is apparently reconciled, but not easily; she makes no verbal concession, and her last speech in the scene is this: 'Your dog or hawk should be rewarded better/ Than I have been. I'll speak not one word more' (lines 189–90).

Bracciano resents her, but cannot resist her. Is Webster's point that beautiful women grow tired of the automatic responses their charms elicit from their menfolk? It would be possible to play it so on stage, but the text seems less committed, as though Vittoria might just as easily be harassed, exhausted or bored as enjoying a moment of vision.

The allure of the female is also represented in Eve, from Adam's point of view the 'last and best/Of all God's works' (Book IX, lines 896–7). Her beauty, like Vittoria's, is irresistible even to Satan, who finds her 'Veiled in a cloud of fragrance', Eden's 'fairest unsupported flower' (lines 425, 432). Her 'graceful innocence' (line 459) overcomes him for a time:

> That space the evil one abstracted stood
> From his own evil, and for the time remained
> Stupidly good…
> (lines 463–5)

It is only when he is reminded that the pleasure he takes in her is 'not for him ordained' (line 470) that he can recollect himself. Her physical attractiveness to Adam proves to be even more damaging for humankind. When he realizes Eve's crime, he concludes that they must suffer the consequences together: 'Our state cannot be severed, we are one,/One flesh; to lose thee were to lose myself' (lines 958–9).

Romantic as his attachment might be, it constitutes disobedience to God equal to Eve's own. Her sin was for her own gain; his seems nobler, but Milton's text charges him that he was 'fondly overcome with female charm' (line 999): his Fall – and our own – is his own fault, but traceable back to the womanly allure of Eve. Milton is less interested than Webster in showing how female thoughts can acquire a dangerous and intriguing independence in the midst of a sexually charged debate. Adam's hapless if chivalric submission to Eve nails both male and female down to joint responsibility in bringing sin (and death) into the world.

Vittoria's last scene sees her still trying her best to find security in a dangerous, patriarchal world, but looking increasingly desperate. Her reaction to Bracciano's torment and death is all about her own situation – 'I am lost for ever' (Act 5, Scene 3, line 34). Her plot with Zanche to outlive Flamineo is a theatrical *tour de force*, and gives us the remarkable spectacle of the two women trampling on him in the mistaken belief that they have shot him dead. This violence and triumphalism from Vittoria is yet another aspect to be accommodated into her chameleon character. Her bravery facing death is what we might expect having seen her in the arraignment, but her ensuing uncertainty is new, and gives her something in common with her brother who dies 'in a mist' (Act 5, Scene 6, line 262)[13]: 'My soul, like to a ship in a black storm,/Is driven I know not whither' (lines 250–51).

These might seem fitting as last words for a woman who has lived dangerously, exploited others and tried to keep ahead of the game, living up to her character as the 'White Devil'. However, her actual last words are relatively tame and disappointing, and might have been given to any of a range of characters 'on the make': 'O happy they that never saw the court,/Nor ever knew great man but by report' (lines 263–4).

---

13 Bosola in *The Duchess of Malfi* also dies 'In a mist' (Act 5, Scene 5, line 94). Webster often imagines death as terminal bad weather.

In this way, Vittoria ends on a kind of anti-climax – a statement that she might have done better with a quieter life. Despite the fact that Webster is writing a tragedy, a genre measured by its end, there is an unfinished quality to her story. Milton, who still has three books to go, is bound to break off Book IX with Eve's attitude to her Fall still in process of formation, and Adam and Eve joined in disobedience and recrimination: he wishes she had listened to him in the first place; she blames him for letting her do what she wanted, in an argument that seems like the easy way out for a woman in a patriarchal society: 'Hadst thou been firm and fixed in thy dissent,/ Neither had I transgressed, nor thou with me' (lines 1160–61).

Adam and Eve finish the book in 'mutual accusation', 'neither self-condemning' (lines 1187–8); the end of the epic poem itself sees them in better accord, but is still only a beginning for them, as they take their 'solitary way' hand in hand out of Paradise.

Thus Webster offers snapshots of Vittoria, both a victim and exploiter of patriarchal society, providing very little in the way of explanation of her behaviour; Milton, after showing little glimmers of false independence in Eve, reduces both lovers, chivalrous patriarch and proto-feminist, to a self-seeking marital quarrel, in which the most important thing is to argue that you are right. Eve, who seems to know her mind better than Vittoria, speaks out, both before and after her Fall; Vittoria can only try on various theatrical roles, none of which fits her exactly, and dies still brutally uncertain who she is and where she is going.

Further reading
Milton
Anna Baldwin, ed., *John Milton: Paradise Lost Book IX*, Oxford Student Texts edition (2008)
Anna Beer, *John Milton: Poet, Pamphleteer and Patriot* (biography) (2008)
Dennis Danielson, ed., *The Cambridge Companion to Milton* (2009)
Alastair Fowler, ed., *Paradise Lost*, Longman Annotated English Poets edition (2007)
Margaret Kean, ed., *John Milton's Paradise Lost: A Sourcebook* (2005)
Nicholas McDowell and Nigel Smith, *The Oxford Handbook of Milton* (2009)
Christopher Ricks, *Milton's Grand Style* (1963)

Webster
John Russell Brown, ed., *The White Devil*, Revels Student Edition (1996)
Jackie Moore, ed., *John Webster: The White Devil*, Oxford Student Texts edition (2011)
Emma Smith, 'Webster, *The Duchess of Malfi*' Oxford University *Great Writers Inspire* podcast (2012), accessible via https://writersinspire.org
Simon Trussler, *Faber Pocket Guide to Elizabethan and Jacobean Drama* (2006)
Stanley Wells, *Shakespeare and Co* (2006)

The Value of Ambiguity in John Webster's *The White Devil* and Andrew Marvell's *Selected Poems*

Peter Doughty

There are various ways of comparing texts of different genres, as other approaches in this collection demonstrate: by reference to contexts, to common concerns, to contemporary ideas or issues. In this essay I intend to explore ways in which *The White Devil* and some of Marvell's poems generate their particular effects. Some means and effects are peculiar to the genre of each; some, however, are similar in perhaps unexpected ways. I approach my analysis through the term *ambiguity*, as employed in William Empson's *Seven Types of Ambiguity* (1935), one of the most influential critical texts of the last century:

> I propose to use the word 'ambiguity' in an extended sense, and shall think relevant to my subject any verbal nuance, however slight, which gives room for alternative reactions to the same piece of language.

As Empson intimates here, ambiguity is a useful term because it can be employed in different ways and contexts, while always retaining the sense of pointing to 'alternative reactions', responses or readings.

A good example of 'a verbal nuance... which gives room for alternative reactions to the same piece of language' is the title of Webster's play. The conventional literal and moral opposition of meanings between the words *white* and *devil* taken separately is not challenged (both words recur, clear in meaning, several times in the play), but by bringing them together the title sets up a relation between them that is ambiguous in the sense I am using: as the words jostle, this ambiguity suggests that, in judging character and the kind of experience explored in the play, neither term is appropriate individually; both meanings have to be held in the mind simultaneously. The presentation of Vittoria (presumably the 'white devil') in the text is correspondingly ambiguous. Catherine Thompson, in her essay on Webster and Milton in this collection, points out that 'she scarcely seems to sustain the same character from one of her few scenes to the next'. Catherine Belsey argues that aspects of Vittoria's characterization typify 'the radically discontinuous subject-positions'[1] that represent femininity in Jacobean drama, some of which seriously undermine masculine dominance. Travis Bogard suggests, in a useful formulation, that by manipulating her presentation in this way Webster intended 'to baffle

---

1 Catherine Belsey, *The Subject of Tragedy: Identity and Difference in Renaissance Drama* (1985).

ordinary judgement'[2]. Ian Jack acknowledges the ambiguity of the character in a comment that is itself deeply ambiguous: 'Vittoria is dishonourable: Webster simply makes her behave as if she were honourable'[3]. In production, the character may be played in a way that represents the ambiguities of the written text, or the multiple aspects may be resolved into a singular reading, as in Frank Dunlop's landmark production for the National Theatre in 1969:

> Dominating the whirlwind from the moment of her long solo first walk across the stage is Geraldine McEwan as Vittoria, her frail body and naked back enveloped by a cobra-hood, her face evil with the mixed satiety and appetite, leer and snigger, coquetry and indecency, of the consummate whore.[4]

A character similarly ambiguous to Vittoria is evident in Marvell's poem 'The Gallery': the speaker presents his mistress alternately as *white* (as Aurora, she 'stretches out her milky thighs', and she is 'Like Venus in her pearly boat') and also as a *devil* (an 'inhuman murderess' and 'Like an enchantress... dost rave/Over [the lover's] entrails'). The portraits of Clora held in the mind of the speaker illustrate that Belsey's 'radically discontinuous subject-positions' typify women presented in poetry as well as drama. Marvell's speaker prefers the *white* version. By choosing to disregard Clora's equally characteristic dark side (or resolving the ambiguity by filtering out one of its terms) you feel the speaker is heading for trouble in any relationship with her. There's an interesting parallel here with Bracciano in *The White Devil*: early in the play he seems to control Vittoria's choices, until he's demoralized by her onslaught in the house of convertites and soon becomes a victim himself – which may be the fate of Marvell's speaker too.

There's a similar Marvellian ambiguity in the speaker's presentation of the child in 'The Picture of Little T.C. in a Prospect of Flowers' as the 'innocent' young girl –

> See with what simplicity
> This nymph begins her golden days!
> In the green grass she loves to lie

and 'the virtuous enemy of man' she is expected to become:

> Yet this is she whose chaster laws
> The wanton Love shall one day fear,

---

2   Quoted by Ann Rosalind Jones in David Scott Kastan and Peter Stallybrass, eds, *Staging the Renaissance* (1991).

3   Ian Jack, 'The Case of John Webster' in R.V. Holdsworth, ed., Casebook Series, *The White Devil and the Duchess of Malfi* (1975).

4   From a review of Frank Dunlop's production for the National Theatre, 1969.

And, under her command severe,
See his bow broke and ensigns torn.

This, one of the most contested of Marvell's poems, has also been read as a comment on contemporary politics and on contemporary methods of gardening. The representation of sex as a battle parallels 'To His Coy Mistress'. The threat that T.C. will die if she doesn't look after her garden properly carries with it the shadow of mortality, particularly since we know, as Marvell certainly did, that the real T.C.'s sister died very young.

If we turn to ways in which male characters are constructed by Webster and Marvell – Flamineo, and Cromwell in the 'Horatian Ode' – we find similarly ambiguous presentations. Who, for instance, is the central figure in *The White Devil*? Traditionally, the central figure in revenge drama[5] is the revenger (for example, Hamlet in Shakespeare's play of that name; Hieronimo, avenging the cowardly murder of his son in *The Spanish Tragedy*; Vindice – the name means *revenge* – who opens *The Revenger's Tragedy* by explaining his project to avenge the murder of his fiancée) and the action of the play charts the progress of the revenge narrative. In Webster's play, however, the pattern is varied; Flamineo is not straightforwardly a revenge figure but nevertheless has peculiar status in *The White Devil*: he appears in more scenes than any other character; has more to say than any of them; is provided with a fuller history of expected gain from great men and inevitable disappointment at their hands; and, unsurprisingly, frequently deplores social inequities. He acts as commentator on exchanges between other characters, and he has more personal addresses to the audience than anyone else. To this extent, he is the main focalizing device in the text[6]. He is also the only figure to develop any moral sense (although only at the end of the play and very briefly); after Cornelia's lament for her son Marcello, Flamineo muses:

I have a strange thing in me, to th'which
I cannot give a name, without it be
Compassion
(Act 5, Scene 4, lines 115–7)

---

5 'Revenge dramas' were elaborately plotted plays, very popular on the Elizabethan and Jacobean stage. The trail-blazing play was *Gorboduc* (1561); the most influential was probably Thomas Kyd's *The Spanish Tragedy* (before 1592). Important revenge plays were written by Marlowe, Shakespeare, Marston, Middleton, Webster and Ford. *The Revenger's Tragedy* (c. 1606), long ascribed to Cyril Tourneur, is now generally accepted to be by Middleton. Such plays usually involve a bloody climax as victims, would-be revengers and avengers of revengers meet in the final scene. Many of the plays, including *The White Devil*, seem to pastiche the form as they exploit it.

6 Focalization is the presentation of a scene through the subjective perception of a character.

And he dies with a degree of self-recognition ("Tis well yet there's some goodness in my death,/My life was a black charnel', Act 5, Scene 6, lines 271–2). The mental state of the victim at death is always a significant indicator in revenge drama, though critics do not always agree on its meaning. Some, like Frank Whigham, find in Flamineo's last moments evidence of the 'struggle to gain or constitute or achieve personal identity'[7]. Others, like Jonathan Dollimore, have been less convinced. For him Flamineo's career and his dying rhetoric constitutes 'Transgression without Virtue', an act of 'stubborn, mindless self-affirmation'[8]. On the one hand, then, in death as in life, Flamineo has features that attract sympathy from the audience or reader. On the other hand, his dark side predominates. He is devious, disloyal, self-pitying, self-justifying and ruthless in pursuit of his own interest, scornful of all bonds of relationship and moral principles, vindictive and murderous. Edward Woodward's playing of Flamineo in the 1969 National Theatre production projected both aspects of the character, playing humorously with the audience in asides and soliloquies but also turning intemperate and vicious as required by the narrative; whereas Gale Edwards's RSC production in 1996 featured a less unambiguous version of the character: 'The sneering, salivating Flamineo of Richard McCabe, pimping for his married sister.'[9]

Thus in *The White Devil* we have little sense of Webster's reading of Flamineo's character, but some sense of his interior life, albeit open to different interpretations. Marvell, determined to keep his personal feelings and opinion out of direct light, and employing personae that are themselves often ambiguous, is even more inscrutable. In 'An Horatian Ode upon Cromwell's Return from Ireland' the intent of the speaking voice is doubly, perhaps even triply, masked. The attitude of the speaker to the leading parliamentarian general is ambiguous; the presentation of his achievements is enigmatic and/or ironic; and views of his temperament and motives are speculative (marked by ifs, buts and rhetorical questions). Marvell introduces a further level of ambiguity by relating his poem, by its title, to a classical poetic tradition of celebrating great leaders as exemplified in Horace's Odes to the Emperor Augustus[10].

---

7   Frank Whigham, *Seizures of the Will in Early English Drama* (1996).

8   Jonathan Dollimore, '*The White Devil*: Transgression without virtue', in Richard Wilson & Richard Dutton, eds, *New Historicism and Renaissance Drama* (1992).

9   From a review of Gale Edwards's production for the RSC, 1996.

10 Augustus Caesar gradually assumed the title and role of first Emperor of the Roman Empire after he defeated Mark Antony during the civil war of 31–30 BCE. Marvell's poem, with its elusive view of Cromwell's rise to power, glances not only at the ambiguity of Horace's *Odes* towards the Emperor Augustus (particularly I and IV) but also at Lucan's equally ambiguous view of power in his account of the Roman civil wars between victorious Julius Caesar and defeated Pompey the Great in the *Pharsalia* (61–5 CE).

As a result:

> The 'Horatian Ode' is undoubtedly one of the most provocatively equivocal poems in English literature. It has been read both as a straightforward encomium of Cromwell and as an ironic deprecation. There is plentiful evidence for both extremes as well as for intermediate positions.[11]

Celebrating Cromwell's return from his campaign (1649–50) to end the Irish resistance to the newly established republic in England, the poem insists on Cromwell's power as a force of nature ('Urgèd his active star... His fiery way divide... burning through the air he went') and also as the 'forcèd pow'r' of history: after the Irish comes the turn of the Scots to be hunted down by Cromwell (the 'falcon') and his army, and beyond that there is no apparent horizon to his ambitions (Cromwell 'to all states not free/Shall climacteric be'). The poem equivocates about both the historical process, acknowledged as inevitable if not altogether to be welcomed, and the nature of the man who is presented as its driving force. Along with his strength of will, Cromwell is ascribed personal virtue and humility in the poem, not, however, by the Commons who benefited from the campaign ('He to the Commons' feet presents/A kingdom, for his first year's rents') but ironically by the Irish, against whom the brutality of Cromwell's campaign was well known[12]:

> They can affirm his praises best,
> And have, though overcome, confessed
> How good he is, how just,
> And fit for highest trust

And the success of the republican rebellion is questioned in both its process and its effect:

> To ruin the great work of time,
> And cast the kingdoms old
> Into another mould.

> Though Justice against Fate complain,
> And plead the ancient rights in vain;
> But those do hold or break,
> As men are strong or weak.

---

11 From the biography for Andrew Marvell available in full via the Poetry Foundation website.

12 The Siege of Drogheda in 1649, which ended in Cromwell's massacre of many of its defenders, and the sack of Wexford a month later, where apparently uncontrolled Parliamentarian soldiers slaughtered the garrison after it had surrendered, are two of the most notorious atrocities in Irish history.

Strength, not justice, determines history. The account of Charles I's dignified behaviour at his execution can be read either as the emotional centre of the poem, or as a structural digression. Nevertheless its effect, for most readers, is to underline that the forces of historical necessity and Cromwell's individual strength converge upon a humble victim on a 'tragic scaffold'; and the diction points to personal qualities the opposite of Cromwell's. The poem's achievement is in a sense negative, in that it privileges no explicit judgement of Cromwell, presenting, like the display in 'The Gallery', a series of alternative views and comparisons from which no attempt emerges to select, or extrapolate, what 'likes me best'.

Both Webster and Marvell were aware of their membership of a community of writers. In his address 'To the Reader' attached to *The White Devil*, Webster lists admiringly fellow playwrights, 'wishing what I write may be read by their light'. Webster liked to weave elements from other writers into his own drama, and members of his audiences might recognize echoes of earlier plays: from *Hamlet* (c. 1601), for example, Flamineo's affected 'distraction', and Cornelia's echoes of Ophelia in her lament after Marcello's murder; perhaps the episode of Flamineo 'dying' twice in the final act is an echo of Kyd's *The Spanish Tragedy*, where characters taking roles in the play-within-a-play do actually die when the figures they are performing are 'killed'. For the readers or audiences who recognized them, echoes of this kind would give rise to Empson's 'alternative reactions to the same piece of language'. The play also echoes effects introduced earlier. Flamineo's doubled 'death' is the obvious example of such a double-take. Subtler effects derive from the relation between the episodes when first Bracciano and then Isabella forswear sharing their marriage bed; this 'divorce' becomes a parody of the wedding service when they swear the same oath: 'Henceforth I'll never lie with thee, by this,/This wedding-ring' (Act 2 Scene 1, lines 193–4; see lines 252–3).

Marvell's writing community had deeper roots than Webster's. In 1921 T.S. Eliot wrote that 'Marvell's best verse is the product of European, that is to say, Latin, culture'[13] and we have seen some evidence elsewhere – in the 'Horatian Ode', as well as in Lynn Robson's essay in this collection, where she writes of his modification of Petrarchan ideals – of the sense that he wrote in response to long-established literary traditions. His 'pastoral' poems, for example may be read as testing the conventions of the genre against the 'real life' of contemporary conditions. The Mower figure is a cross between traditional 'grim reaper' and pastoral gardener complaining about new methods of horticulture. 'Upon Appleton House' takes off from the tradition of 'country house' or 'garden' poems, of which Ben Jonson's 'To Penshurst' is the classic example, but complicates the genre by exploring a variety of contemporary issues arising from the Civil War. 'The Garden' reinterprets the Genesis story, arguing that

---

13 T.S. Eliot, 'Andrew Marvell', reprinted in *Selected Essays* (1932). Eliot, major modernist poet, is also arguably the most influential literary critic of the first half of the twentieth century.

Adam was better off before Eve ever appeared. Like scenes in *The White Devil* the poems resonate with their precursors in the mind of the alert reader.

If read in this way Marvell's best-known poem, 'To His Coy Mistress', provides a range of 'alternative reactions to the same piece of language'. It may be familiar from anthologies of love poetry, but readers rarely agree about either its tone or meaning. Eliot's account of the poem (and of Marvell in general), which appeared in 1921, stresses its 'traditional' qualities, rather than its uniqueness:

> The theme is one of the great traditional commonplaces of European literature. It is the theme of *O mistress mine*, of *Gather ye rosebuds*, of *Go lovely rose*; it is in the savage austerity of Lucretius and the intense levity of Catullus.

'O mistress mine', one of Feste's songs from *Twelfth Night* (c. 1601), in the tradition of *carpe diem* ('seize the day') poems, ends like this:

> What is love? 'Tis not hereafter,
> Present mirth hath present laughter:
> What's to come is still unsure.
> In delay there lies no plenty,
> Then come kiss me, sweet-and-twenty;
> Youth's a stuff will not endure.[14]

The opening lines of each section of Marvell's poem, less domestic but equally lyrical, maintain the diction and the sentiment of this tradition. The first section then stretches space and time hyperbolically, straddling a global east-west separation and evoking a sexual encounter lasting the whole of human history, from the humorously specific 'ten years before the flood' to the future 'conversion of the Jews'[15]. The remainder of the second section, after the conventional reminder of time, challenges the coy mistress with threats from a very different kind of discourse, gathering up physical/material realities of mortality ('marble vault... worms shall try... honour turn to dust... into ashes all my lust') into a *memento mori*

---

14 The poems Eliot compares with 'To His Coy Mistress' are by respectively Shakespeare (*Twelfth Night* Act 2, Scene 3), Robert Herrick and Edmund Waller. All make use, like 'To His Coy Mistress', of the *carpe diem* motif, reminding us that time is short and we should make immediate use of it. The phrase is best known from Horace's *Odes* 1:11 (c. 30 BCE), but the idea behind it was already a poetic commonplace. Both Catullus (84–54 BCE) and Lucretius (99–55 BCE), also mentioned by Eliot, were Roman poets of the Late Republic. Catullus wrote a number of lyric poems on the *carpe diem* theme, of which the best known is V, *Vivamus, mea Lesbia* (We should live, my Lesbia). Lucretius argues in *De Rerum Natura* that supernatural beliefs are illusory, death ends all life and the fear of death is therefore irrational.

15 This phrase is code for time that cannot be calculated.

harangue more appropriate for a Calvinist[16] fire-and-brimstone sermon than an invitation to intimacy. The language of the final section, again after opening lines of complimentary playfulness, takes an even more extraordinary turn, signalled by the rhyming of 'may' with 'birds of prey', generating a crescendo of aggression and violence. Other Marvell poems use imagery of battle to characterize sexual relationships: the 'bow broke and ensigns torn' of 'The Picture of Little T.C.' and, in 'Daphnis and Chloe':

> He, well-read in all the ways
> By which men their siege maintain,
> Knew not that the fort to gain
> Better 'twas the siege to raise.

In 'To His Coy Mistress' the prospect is that the siege of this resisting fortification is to be concluded by the deployment of heavy artillery, the cannonball fired 'Thorough the iron gates of life' that guard the lady's 'quaint honour' and 'long preserved virginity'. The particular overall effect of this poem arises from its ambiguous relation to a poetic tradition that it repeatedly mimics, but also satirizes, undermines, and finally explodes. Local ambiguities also abound in the poem: the use of 'coy' implies that the mistress is playing a game of hard-to-get; and in the disturbing prediction, 'worms shall try/That long preserved virginity', 'try' has the meaning of 'put to the test' and 'preserved' contains the meaning of 'salted', 'sugared' or even 'pickled' as well as 'protected'. Such 'alternative reactions to the same piece[s] of language' throughout challenge the poem's traditional status as a love poem at all, as Gordon Campbell advises:

> any woman who could be seduced by such a poem would be a half-wit incapable of enjoying bathetic effects such as the juxtaposition of the Ganges and the Humber. The implied reader of the poem may be the object of the poet's erotic intentions but the real readers of such poems were male, and the poem rests on shared male assumptions about women as consumable sexual commodities.[17]

However, it may be that in the poem Marvell is in fact satirizing not only earlier versions of the *carpe diem* theme, but also the kind of reader who does share such assumptions.

---

16 Calvinists were (and are) followers of the pastor and theologian John Calvin (1509–64), who argued (among other things) that God had pre-destined some human souls to be saved and others to be damned before the creation of the world. Most Calvinists considered themselves saved ('of the elect'), so some extremists envisaged lurid torments for those not so fortunate.

17 Gordon Campbell, introduction to Everyman selection of *Andrew Marvell* (1997).

As a further example of the wide range of alternative readings, another account (by Francis Barker) approaches the poem as a process of dismemberment, noting that the heart, last mentioned in the poem's catalogue of body parts, 'scattered across the text in discrete pieces' was also the organ 'so often held aloft to one audience or another gathered at the foot of the public scaffold, dramatic or penal'[18]. The extraordinary achievement of the poem, characteristic of Marvell, is that so many possible meanings are simultaneously available.

Little is known of Webster's biography; mostly, there are details of his theatre activities. We know much more about Marvell's life, though mysteries remain. Nigel Smith's 2010 biography has the title *Andrew Marvell: The Chameleon*, an appropriate term to cover the 'gallery' of roles and identities attributed to him (such as friend of members of the Cavalier party before the Civil War, private tutor, civil servant under Cromwell's Protectorate, patriot, spy, conspirator, possibly even concealed homosexual, MP for Hull after the Restoration, father to Whig politics and the liberal tradition, satirical pamphleteer and freethinker). The word so often now applied to him is 'amphibian', no doubt picking up the image of the 'rational amphibii' at the end of his most ambitious poem, 'Upon Appleton House', but also no doubt glancing at his sexuality, or elusive political views. As a poet, *amphibian* (or *chameleon*) is exactly the right description for him – for his performances in several poetic genres, each in an adopted voice, gesturing within and between poems towards often contradictory positions and opinions, but unequivocal about none.

Further reading
Webster
Sandra Clark, *John Webster: The White Devil and The Duchess of Malfi* (1987)
Andrew McRae, *Renaissance Drama* (2003)
Jackie Moore, ed., *John Webster: The White Devil*, Oxford Student Texts edition (2011)
Gamini Salgado, introduction to *Three Jacobean Tragedies* (1969)
T.F. Wharton, *Moral Experiment in Jacobean Drama* (1996)

Marvell
Anna Beer, ed., *Andrew Marvell: Selected Poems*, Oxford Student Texts edition (2012)
John Carey, ed, *Andrew Marvell*, Penguin Critical Anthologies (1969)
Christopher Hill, *The World Turned Upside Down: Radical Ideas During The English Revolution* (1972)
Derek Hirst and Steven N. Zwicker, eds, *The Cambridge Companion to Andrew Marvell* (2011)
Dianne Purkiss, *Literature, Gender and Politics During the English Civil War* (2005)
Nigel Smith, *Andrew Marvell: The Chameleon* (2010)

---

18 Francis Barker, 'Into the Vault', in Thomas Healy, ed., *Andrew Marvell: A Longman Critical Reader* (1998).

Order versus Decadence: John Ford's *'Tis Pity She's a Whore* and Andrew Marvell's *Selected Poems*

Lynn Robson

> The heavens themselves, the planets and this centre
> Observe degree, priority and place...
> Take but degree away, untune that string,
> And, hark, what discord follows!
> William Shakespeare, *Troilus and Cressida*, Act 1, Scene 3

John Ford (c. 1586– after 1639) and Andrew Marvell (1621–78) lived in a society that prized order[1]: as Shakespeare's Ulysses says in the quotation above, if the universe is not carefully structured according to 'degree, priority and place' then what follows is 'discord'. His words refer to belief in a Great Chain of Being. In this representation of a strictly hierarchical physical and spiritual universe, God (who is perfection) sits at the top in heaven, and all matter and life he has created is ordered beneath him as follows: angels, humans, birds, wild animals, domesticated animals, trees and other plants, precious stones, metals and minerals, with hell and demons at the bottom. Humankind is placed between the angels and the animals and has the capacities of both. In early modern thinking, the 'brute' part of humankind – what Soranzo in *'Tis Pity She's a Whore* calls the 'lust-belepered body' (Act 4, Scene 3, line 61) – is governed by base, unreasoning passions which tie it to mortality and the earth. Humans' rational part, the soul, is at one with the angels and draws them towards immortality in heaven. The irony of this, as Marvell points out, is that body and soul are 'fettered' and 'manacled' together, 'A soul hung up, as 'twere, in chains/Of nerves, and arteries, and veins' ('A Dialogue between the Soul and Body'), and there is constant friction between the necessity that keeps them together and the desire to be apart.

Humanity's position in the Great Chain of Being expresses the potential for both order and decadence. Although the noun 'decadence' originates from the nineteenth century, its definition of 'a state of decay or decline' or a 'falling off' from excellence or vitality (*Oxford English Dictionary*) would have been familiar to Ford and Marvell, who understood that humans were made decadent by the Fall and original sin. They would probably have used the adjective 'degenerate' to express the

---

1 This essay broadly reflects a new historicist approach to the study of literature, in which literary texts are put in dialogue with the most significant developments in the history of ideas. New historicism emerged as a significant way of reading literature in the early 1990s and continues to influence literary studies. This essays considers both texts and how they show that older concepts of the Great Chain of Being and the Petrarchan ideal were increasingly challenged by the intellectual and imaginative approach to the English Civil War.

sense that perfection in earthbound, fleeting human life was impossible; perfection and immortality were found only in heaven. This perspective means that anything humans might produce is inevitably tainted and faulty. So the idea of the Great Chain of Being is merely a human *attempt* to represent a divinely instituted order – it approximates to a divine truth but cannot be literally true.

For Ford and Marvell, rhetoric was a linguistic structure that allowed them to order and express human experience. They inherited its traditions from a hierarchy of authoritative writers (including Roman writers and previous generations of English poets such as Chaucer, Sidney, Spenser and Shakespeare) that legitimized their own works and provided them with a set of stock stories, styles and imagery. Poets could create illusory worlds that might briefly offer an escape from the fallen human one, but they did so knowing that their golden worlds only revealed their own decadence because the serpent will always be in Eden. Marvell writes in 'The Coronet' of:

> the serpent old
> That, twining in his speckled breast,
> About the flow'rs disguised does fold

The speaker imagines a coronet of flowers as a gift for Christ that will replace the crown of thorns, but he also knows it is crafted from a garland of inadequate rhetorical flourishes that reveal the futility of his aspiration. Poetry can expose illusions of perfection as false, but is a dangerous place for poets and readers who give into its temptation, indulging themselves in its fantasies.

Both writers, though separated by a generation and adopting different genres, order their writing by the conventions of a shared literary heritage, including those of Petrarchan poetry[2]. Petrarchan conventions demand the elevation of an unattainable ideal to near divine status, particularly a female beloved who is imagined as cold, distant, cruel and the 'property' of another man. The languishing poet/lover is haunted by her disdain and his all-consuming desire: he adores her, but cannot have her. In *'Tis Pity She's a Whore* (1630–33) Ford challenges these conventions by exposing the decadence of idolatry lurking within them, while Marvell's poetry of the late 1640s and 1650s considers whether or not they are so devalued that they cannot express a world turned upside down by civil war, in which the structure of hierarchical monarchy had disappeared at the moment of Charles I's beheading.

Ford demonstrates these dangers throughout *'Tis Pity She's a Whore*. The Friar's opening lines indicate that Giovanni and he are midway through an argument. University has made Giovanni a skilled rhetorician, full of 'school-points', who excels in academic disputation. Giovanni's studies have disrupted his perception of

---

2   Petrarch (Francesco Petrarca) 1304–74, Italian humanist scholar and poet whose sonnets were first translated into English in the 1530s by Sir Thomas Wyatt and the Earl of Surrey.

the Great Chain of Being, so that rather than 'bless the sun' and God who created it, he would rather 'reason why it shines' (line 10). However, Giovanni's reasoning has led him to replace one ideal, worship for God, with another, worship for his sister. He believes the stereotypical Petrarchan imagery that would say that Annabella's beauty makes her divine:

> Must I not praise
> That beauty, which if framed anew, the gods
> Would make a god of...
> (Act 1, Scene 1, lines 20–22)

His understanding is disordered because Annabella's beauty, created by God, should only be interpreted as proof of God's existence. The decadence of Giovanni's idolatry (because he worships the image instead of the thing itself) is emphasized when he explains that he desires to be 'One soul, one flesh, one love, one heart, one all' with Annabella (line 34), language that rightly belongs to the Christian marriage service. There is no doubt that Giovanni has fallen from the admired order of what the Friar calls the 'government, behaviour, learning, speech,/Sweetness, and all that could make up a man!' (lines 51–2).

Giovanni creates his sister as an idol through the language and imagery of Petrarchan poetry, and the play shows that such habits are infectious. Soranzo – Giovanni's rival – enters the play reading a 'smooth licentious poet'[3] but saying that he prefers the humanist[4] 'mean' of (measured) experience, appearing to reject the Petrarchan 'extreme'. However, by praising Annabella's 'diviner cheeks' and pining for a single glance from her, Soranzo shows that he is also trapped by stereotypical literary perceptions of love and women (Act 2, Scene 2, lines 1–17).

The idealizing language shared by Giovanni, Soranzo and the poets who absorb them transforms the speaker into creator and owner of the object being described and in Petrarchan poetry that 'object' is invariably a woman. Giovanni and Soranzo want sexual possession of Annabella, and the only language they have to indicate it is that of idolatry. If you make an idol you can destroy it and, as fallen humans are unable to live up to expectations of perfection, destruction is as violent as it is inevitable. Soranzo's castigation of Annabella as 'strumpet, famous whore' with a 'corrupted bastard-bearing womb' (Act 4, Scene 3, lines 1, 14) is anticipated in the language of Hippolita's lament in Act 2. She describes how Soranzo's 'tears' and 'oaths' broke through the order of her chastity, reputation and armoured 'heart

---

3 Jacopo Sannazaro, 1458–1530.

4 Humanism was an intellectual and cultural movement in which scholars, educators and civic leaders focused on the study of grammar, rhetoric, history, poetry and moral philosophy, engaging in the translation of ancient Greek and Latin texts.

of steel' (Act 2, Scene 2, lines 36–7). Accepting and believing his blasphemous protestations of worship have led to Hippolita's rejection and resulted in 'loss of womanhood… hatred and contempt' (lines 41–2). The words of Soranzo's spurned mistress expose, just as clearly as Soranzo's own brutality, the hypocritical, decadent double standard that lies at the heart of Petrarchan poetics.

Marvell's lyrics participate in similar poetic games but with a different tone. He looks back to the literary traditions of classical pastoral as well as those of the 1620s and 1630s (when *'Tis Pity* was written) when it was possible to believe that a poet might convince a reader that language and imagery can create an ordered world. In 'The Unfortunate Lover', the speaker gazes on ghostly figures in a Petrarchan landscape – 'Alas, how pleasant are their days' – as 'Sorted by pairs', lovers flit by 'fountains cool, and shadows green'. However, they are as short-lived as 'meteors of a summer night' and too insubstantial to 'make impression upon Time'. There may have been a literary time when a poet/lover could pretend that he would spend 'a hundred years' in praising his mistress's eyes and devote 'thirty thousand to the rest' ('To His Coy Mistress'), but such barren idolatry leads only to a 'marble vault' and fruitless longing. Lovers are subservient to the time that will destroy them. In the same poem the speaker finds it is pleasurable but decadent to imagine his mistress finding rubies by the Ganges; it is better to admit the pretence, succumb to desire, taste the sweetness, and agree that most human experience of love is ordered by the inevitability that he will 'complain' by the Humber[5].

For all their wit and nostalgia, Marvell's speakers are as obsessed with sexual possession as Giovanni and Soranzo. The speaker in 'To His Coy Mistress' is candid about his desire to beat the worms to that 'long preserved virginity'. In 'The Gallery', the speaker gazes on a series of portraits of his beloved Clora that depict similar contradictory, damaging stereotypes of femininity to those that Ford explores. Clora is simultaneously 'inhuman murderess', 'Like to Aurora in the dawn', 'enchantress', and 'Venus', depending on where the speaker looks. He finally chooses to concentrate on his first impression of Clora: an idealized portrait of her as 'tender shepherdess' with flowers in her hair and at her breast. This is a deliberate act of seeing and not-seeing: the poet-speaker has 'contrived' the image and his gaze indicates possession but, although he chooses the idealized version, the others are not obliterated – they remain to come into focus when the speaker's (and the reader's) gaze is shifted.

Marvell's objectified women are stereotypically silent, intensifying a sense of forcible, masculine possession. In poetry, the reader's gaze is more easily controlled than in drama, where dialogue is demanded and an audience's eyes can wander across a stage. Ford exploits this potential for multiple perspectives because Annabella must step away from the early modern convention of chaste, silent and

---

5   The river that runs through Marvell's native Hull.

obedient women to speak, act and move. Represented by an actor's body she (even when played by a boy) is more obviously *woman* than any of Marvell's distant female figures. Like a woman in an Elizabethan sonnet sequence[6], Annabella first appears gazing down on Giovanni from above. When she speaks it is clear that far from disdaining him she reciprocates her brother's idolatry: he is a 'celestial creature'. She also sees him as a stereotypical Petrarchan lover with a 'sad aspect' who walks 'careless of himself' (Act 1, Scene 2, lines 138–40). Their mutual, decadent passion is quickly expressed and consummated. They are deeply in love, but the self-destructive power of incest is the inevitable outcome of their disordered perspectives: they see only each other and think their love legitimized by literary conventions that imagine lovers as twin souls. Their obsessive gazing at their reflections in each other's eyes is a representation of sexual union. Giovanni and Annabella indulge in ordered, formal exchanges, echoing each other's vows in yet another perversion of the ritual of Christian marriage:

> ANNABELLA: On my knees,
> Brother, even by our mother's dust, I charge you,
> Do not betray me to your mirth or hate;
> Love me, or kill me, brother.
> GIOVANNI: On my knees,
> Sister, even by my mother's dust I charge you,
> Do not betray me to your mirth or hate;
> Love me, or kill me, sister.
> (Act 1, Scene 2, lines 258–64)

Beginning and ending the vows with a repetition of 'Brother/brother', 'Sister/sister', in addition to echoing one another almost exactly throughout, expresses the destructive claustrophobia of incest. Giovanni alters only a single pronoun – Annabella's *'our* mother' becomes *'my* mother' – emphasizing his masculine opinion that he has a right of possession over his sister. His degradation of an ordered familial hierarchy demonstrates the degree of his decadence.

The destructive force of this is made gruesomely evident at the end of the play when Giovanni cuts out Annabella's heart, spears it on his dagger and displays it to the banqueting citizens and nobles of Parma. Here he makes literal two of the central metaphors of Petrarchan poetry: that love comes when Cupid's arrow pierces a lover's heart causing constant suffering, and that lovers can transplant their hearts

---

6   Sonnet sequences, like those by Sidney, Spenser and Daniel, were very popular in the 1590s. Although the fashion for them declined in the early seventeenth century, the conventions that governed them remained influential on love lyrics generally and on later sonnet writers such as Donne and Milton.

into each other's breasts[7]. The terrible outcome is that finally to possess Annabella and demonstrate the 'truth' of his Petrarchan adoration, Giovanni murders her and their unborn child.

Ironically Giovanni, the active, desiring male lover, is more static than Annabella, who should, in Pertrarchan tradition, be the immobile, venerated statue. However, Annabella challenges such stereotypes. She mocks Soranzo when he assigns her the role of 'chaste disdain', telling him that his 'common sense' should assure him that if she loved him she would tell him so (Act 3, Scene 2, lines 32, 41), and she refuses to fall in with Bergetto's absurd attempts to be her suitor. She also refutes Soranzo's insults when he discovers her pregnancy and offers him the possibility of a relationship based on the order of honour rather than the decadence of passion, and one that is not warped by the idolatrous extremity of the virgin/whore dichotomy. Finally she seeks to escape the disorder of incest and, finding true repentance, dies with a prayer of forgiveness and contrition. From a modern perspective, Annabella's change of heart may be seen as weakness as she bows to external moral pressure. However, early modern audiences are more likely to have understood that, unlike her brother who remains constant to his decadent private religion and dies still worshipping 'Annabella's face' (Act 5, Scene 6, line 111), her soul is bound for the ordered perfection of heaven.

Ford links the decadence of Annabella and Giovanni's incest to wider patterns of civic disorder, showing that incest is not only a symbol of Parma's decadence but also contributes to it. Servants insult noblemen, citizens' expectations of justice are never met and Giovanni's humanist learning is used to seduce his sister rather than contribute to the city's future stability. The inward-looking fantasies of incest and Petrarchanism deny any communication with the world outside, and the Cardinal's corruption of his role as a judge replicates that denial, revealing that he is as decadent as Giovanni. Rather than representing the order of God's justice, the Cardinal protects the guilty Grimaldi solely because he is 'Of princes' blood' and refuses any challenge from the citizens (Act 3, Scene 9, line 58)[8].

In Marvell's lyrics the self-regarding isolation of Petrarchanism also proves impossible to sustain. The world always intrudes on fantasies of self-sufficiency and withdrawal, and in the 1650s it was a world shaped by the 'intestine strife' of a civil war[9]. Marvell looks back to the poetic certainties of pre-Civil War England

---

7   For example Sir Philip Sidney, 'My true-love hath my heart'.

8   Ford's treatment of the Cardinal as a corrupt figure fits in with the anti-Catholic prejudice of much early modern drama, including Webster's *The White Devil* and *The Duchess of Malfi.*

9   The Civil War lasted from 1642–9, ending with the execution of Charles I. A Commonwealth (republic) and then Protectorate (under Oliver Cromwell) followed before the monarchy was restored under Charles II in 1660. Contemporary texts use the vivid phrase 'intestine strife' to depict a country destroying itself from within.

and reflects on their deficiencies. Conventionally, nymphs lived in ideal natural landscapes that were full of flowers; 'flowers' was the word used by early modern writers to describe the images with which they decorated their poems; flowers can be made into 'poesies', and 'poesy' was a synonym for 'poetry', which is why, in 'The Coronet', Marvell writes 'I gather flow'rs (my fruits are only flow'rs)'. So when Marvell writes about gardens, as in 'The Garden' and 'The Mower' poems, he is also writing about the writing of poetry. The language and imagery Marvell uses to create the world of 'The Nymph Complaining for the Death of her Fawn' (one of the most notoriously difficult poems to explicate in his canon) recalls the literary style that was most fashionable in the 1620s and 1630s, when lyric poets appeared to show unshakeable confidence in the power of poetry to order experience. This was the literary impulse of the leading 'Cavalier poet', Richard Lovelace (1618–57)[10], whose poetry – in which he would 'fairest nymphs approve' – also, Marvell says, 'thawed the most congealèd breast' of reluctant ladies ('To his Noble Friend Mr Richard Lovelace').

However, in 'The Nymph Complaining for the Death of her Fawn', the Nymph has been charmed by lyric voices and her garden, a supposed haven of pastoral perfection, has been invaded twice: once by the faithless Sylvio who brings heartbreak, and then by the 'troopers'[11] who bring death. The beguiling but 'Unconstant Sylvio' seems to belong, like Lovelace, to the poetic world of Charles I's court. His gift of the fawn is made in language that reveals his poetic sterility, as he puns on 'dear' and 'deer', something Thomas Wyatt (one of the first English sonnet writers) was doing back in the 1530s. Marvell contrasts Sylvio's smooth but meaningless Petrarchan commonplaces and counterfeit Cavalier behaviour – 'This waxèd tame, while he grew wild' – with the Nymph's plain but truthful language and heartfelt constancy. Like Ford, Marvell reverses expectations: in Petrarchan tradition, the woman was fickle and the despairing male lover heartbroken but constant.

From this perspective, the fawn's significance has several layers: it is an image of Sylvio's love – when he 'took his heart' he 'Left me his fawn' – but it replaces Sylvio's betrayal with faithfulness and companionship; as an image of unjustly destroyed innocence it represents the Nymph herself (Marvell is careful not to gender the fawn), and it is perfect, 'a wondrous thing'. Marvell consistently emphasizes the fawn's whiteness by comparing it with 'whitest sheets of lilies', 'swans', 'turtles' (doves), and 'milk-white lambs, and ermines pure'. As the Nymph (like Marvell) looks back on a destroyed world of peace and security forged in the absence of

---

10 Richard Lovelace is the author of two well-known anthology poems, 'To Lucasta, Going to the Wars' and 'To Althea, From Prison', both published in 1649.

11 'Trooper' was coined relatively late in the Civil War, entering the language in the late 1640s and referring to Scottish soldiers. It was eventually used to describe any soldier, either Royalist or Parliamentarian.

cruel Petrarchan lovers, she grieves, not only for the fawn's death but also at the impossibility of ever representing it in a way that could convey its perfection and ensure its immortality. The poem opens with the sound of the musket-shot that kills the fawn and ends with the sound of weeping, as the Nymph laments that although she wants the statue of the fawn and herself to be made of 'purest alabaster' it can never approach the fawn's perfection: 'For I would have thine image be/White as I can, though not as thee.'

The fawn is perfect only in the Nymph's memory and imagination. Through his Nymph, Marvell reminds his readers of the decadent lie that art (sculpture or poetry) could ever achieve perfection, but also grieves for the consolation such a view of art might offer. The Nymph, Sylvio and the fawn live in a world of poetic order that has been destroyed with a single shot. In this poem the Civil War has made retreat into poetic gardens impossible.

Ford and Marvell share an understanding of the potential for order and decadence that lies in Petrarchanism. However, the twenty years that separate *'Tis Pity She's a Whore* from Marvell's pre-Restoration poems give the writers different perspectives on that same tradition. At the end of *'Tis Pity* the words and actions of the decadent Cardinal restore order to Parma and, through this device, Ford exposes the paradoxes of his play-world: he shows the dangers of failing to mistrust lies of perfection but does so with lovers who speak sweet and sensitive poetry; the Cardinal's characterization of Annabella as 'whore' has been undermined by the action of the play, but the conventions of Petrarchan idolatry ensure the continuation of the virgin/whore structure. Through a world in which brother and sister regard each other as husband and wife and citizens think themselves the equals of noblemen, the audience must consider different perspectives but the structures (imperfect but human) remain. Humans are necessarily decadent; Italians (because Catholic) offer an exaggerated perspective on this decadence.

Twenty years later, Marvell knows that it is not just the people inhabiting the world that are degenerate but the times themselves, and 'speaking well' ('To his Noble Friend Mr Richard Lovelace') in poetry may no longer be enough. *An Horatian Ode upon Cromwell's Return from Ireland* (1650) opens with the image of a poet longing to stay with his 'Muses dear' and 'sing/His numbers languishing', whose only desire is to gather flowers and make 'poesies' as beautiful as those of his predecessors. The poem makes clear that the only images this poet-speaker might craft are slippery portraits of 'great' men (Oliver Cromwell and Charles I) rather than coy mistresses.

The Civil War has changed the world to the point where it has become unrecognizable when filtered through the lens of Petrarchan traditions. A radical shift in poetic perspective is necessary, and that is exactly what Marvell delivers at the end of one of his most important poems, *Upon Appleton House*. Following a Petrarchan idealization of Maria Fairfax ('Blest Nymph!') that in an earlier time would have been the climax of the poem, Marvell ends instead with the matter-of-fact observation that the world is 'not, what once it was', but a 'rude heap together hurled;/All negligently overthrown'. The clear gradations of the Great Chain of Being, with humans caught between beasts and angels, will no longer do, nor will the artificial elevation of one human over another. Instead Marvell creates the image of 'rational amphibii' who can live in two worlds and *unite* humans and animals. As the night sky, once the repository of ideas about the Great Chain of Being, wheels around the narrator, Marvell replaces idealization with a human perspective drawing imagery from the everyday, the commonplace. 'Let's [go] in', the narrator urges in the final couplet, closing the gap between poet and image, persona and reader, showing that when hierarchies disappear, it is not 'discord' that results but a different kind of sympathy that looks to the future.

Further reading
Critical studies

Anna Beer, ed., *Andrew Marvell: Selected Poems*, Oxford Student Texts edition (2012)

Robyn Bolam, 'John Ford, Mary Wroth, and the Final Scene of *'Tis Pity She's a Whore'* in Michael Hattaway, ed., *A New Companion to English Renaissance Literature and Culture* (2010)

Richard Gill, ed., John Ford: *'Tis Pity She's a Whore*, Oxford Student Texts edition (2012)

Derek Hirst and Stephen N. Zwicker, eds, *The Cambridge Companion to Andrew Marvell* (2011)

N.H. Keeble, ed., *The Cambridge Companion to Writing of the English Revolution* (2001)

Sonia Massai, ed., *'Tis Pity She's a Whore*, Arden Early Modern Drama edition (2011)

Nigel Smith, ed., *The Poems of Andrew Marvell* (2007)

Songs of Innocence and of Experience by William Blake and *The Rivals* by Richard Brinsley Sheridan: Eighteenth-century Civilization Exposed/Celebrated

Julian Thompson

Blake (born 1757) and Sheridan (born 1751) were reasonably close contemporaries. A biographical sketch of each man supplies interesting contrasts. Blake was descended from generations of nonconformists[1] and from London tradesmen. He was self-taught. 'There *is* no use in education,' wrote Blake. 'I hold it wrong – It is the Great Sin.'[2] Are the black-gowned figures 'walking their rounds' in 'The Garden of Love' just 'priests'? Or are they also schoolmasters? Sheridan's Irish roots were pulled up at the age of eight, and as his aspirations were to wealth and influence, so he gravitated naturally to the centres of power and fashion that had grown up since Stuart times in London's West End, notably the theatre and Parliament. He spent a few years at Harrow School[3], but realized early that in the patronage system of late eighteenth-century England who you knew and, particularly, who you impressed was much more important than schooling. As Mrs Malaprop suggests, nine-year-olds were often sent 'to a boarding-school, in order to learn a little ingenuity and artifice' (Act 1, Scene 2, lines 258–9). The young Sheridan picked up plenty. From the beginning he chose words that amused (rather than educated) his showy, sophisticated and influential audience, whether in the theatre or Parliament, and if he taught anybody anything it was usually, as Jack Absolute teaches his father, by means of laughter.

Blake was a man who laughed frequently too, but his works, not the most amusing in the language, have about them a solemn joy that is very like gravitas (for example, the smile of the baby in 'A Cradle Song'). Sheridan's life was measured out in coffee cups, with servants (as long as he had money to pay them) sprinting in every direction, much as Lucy, Fag and David jostle on the edges of his play. His taste was for power: how to obtain it, how to manage it. He graduated from boy-wonder playwright at twenty-three to manage Drury Lane Theatre and fitfully to direct that 'corridor of power'[4], the lobby of the House of

---

1   Those who had objected to the Catholic rituals championed by the High Church party before the Civil War, and who had largely become established as the equivalent of the modern free churches by the end of the seventeenth century.

2   Alexander Gilchrist, *The Life of William Blake* (1863).

3   Harrow School, dating from the sixteenth century, is one of the most prestigious public (privately funded) schools in England.

4   C.P. Snow's phrase.

Commons[5]. It is doubtful whether Blake ever entered the Palace of Westminster, though he lived much of his life within a mile of it. Sheridan knew the vicissitudes of profit and loss, losing his playhouse to fire, his seat in the Commons to a fickle electorate and, stripped of Parliamentary privilege[6], was arrested for debt. Blake moved from one unassuming set of lodgings to another, and worked a twelve- or fourteen-hour day, combining the handwritten texts of his poems with engraved pictorial designs. He could see no reason why poetry and engraving should be viewed as separate disciplines, so he rolled them together, publishing and printing his own texts and his own images, forming a composite image from an inked copper plate that was bound to differ every time it was printed. Perhaps predictably, Sheridan blended politics and theatre, power and amusement, less productively than Blake blended poetry and art.

Both men reacted with strong opposition to the widely held views of their age. They rejected the drearier doctrines of the Enlightenment: that science would one day explain and codify every aspect of human behaviour; that economics, properly understood, would become the motor of politics and desire; and that every philosopher (like David Hume[7]) would come to his deathbed 'hoping nothing – believing nothing – ... And FEARING nothing'[8]. Sheridan's play begs to differ, drawing attention not to the uniformity of his characters but to their quirkiness, their imaginative flights, their delight in hyperbole. What really excites us about the Absolutes, father and son, is their tough, slyly expressed affection for one another, not to mention Sir Anthony's over-statements, which sound so peremptory they divide the globe in half: 'don't enter the same hemisphere with me!' (Act 2, Scene 1, lines 492–3). Lydia, who ought to be caged by the assumptions of her age, the conventions of fashionable Bath and the books she can hire from a circulating library, is that rare eighteenth-century commodity, a feisty bluestocking[9]. Her reading is balanced[10],

---

5　The Members' Lobby of the House of Commons was designed as something like a secretarial space for the working members, where messages and solicitations could be left for them; in Sheridan's time it became proverbially the place where the real business of the House was done.

6　At this time Members of Parliament were routinely granted freedom from arrest on civil charges, such as debt.

7　David Hume (1711–76), the premier British Enlightenment philosopher, conceded that the universe probably did exhibit 'something like design', but that God was a philosophical concept, not a revealed truth.

8　The words are those of the dying atheist, Sergeant Bothwell, in Sir Walter Scott's *Old Mortality* (1816), Chapter 16.

9　An educated woman was at this time known as a 'bluestocking'; however most 'blues' were held to be dowdy and judgemental, rather than vigorous and tolerant, like Lydia.

10　The Edwardian critic George H. Nettleton made extensive study of the twenty books listed in *The Rivals* Act 1, Scene 2, summarizing the insights they give into the tastes and needs of eighteenth-century fashionable society; his essay is reprinted in P.H. Davison, ed., *Sheridan: Comedies* (Macmillan Casebook, 1986).

mixing theological works with Ovid's studies of love and sex[11], and she is quite aware that getting on in late eighteenth-century society has as much to do with manners as philosophy, so she keeps by her the *Letters of Lord Chesterfield to His Son*[12] (Act 1, Scene 2, lines 172–9). Her imagination is both informed and passionate, disposed to question received opinion and to privilege her own unruly (but thoroughly human) desires. It's a shame the play doesn't give her more to do.

Lydia's attitudes to love and sex might be viewed as part of a fresh attitude to the 'natural' (that is, sexual) being that came in with Samuel Richardson's novels[13] and the cult of sensibility (near its peak when Sheridan wrote his play)[14]. It would not be unreasonable to compare the cruel tests she imposes on Jack's love in the freezing January garden with the gloating sexual cruelties explored soon afterwards by the Marquis de Sade[15]. The difference is one of scale, not of kind. Blake, too, knew all about pleasure's inter-relationship with pain in both desire and sexual activity. His 'The Clod and the Pebble' and 'My Pretty Rose Tree' in *Songs of Experience* are masterpieces of compressed psychology, anticipating twentieth-century understanding of sexual power games. Both disdain the repressive or sanctimonious boundaries imposed by contemporary culture. Instead Blake concentrates on showing how we are all exploiters (like Lydia) or (willingly?) exploited (like Jack), and we need one another, as bully needs victim, sadist needs masochist, master needs slave. In the most influential reading of 'Rose Tree' the speaker even seems to get a kick out of his girl's jealousy. The poems also resemble the mind-games (and sex-games) of the greatest of all eighteenth-century novels in English, Samuel Richardson's *Clarissa* (1747–8), where the needs of the characters he has created scorn the novelist's efforts to control them morally. Lydia's library doesn't explicitly include that book, but we can be pretty sure she, like every gutsy Georgian lady, had read it.

---

11 Publius Ovidius Naso (43 BCE –17/18 CE) wrote sophisticated studies of love and mythology, considered both scandalous and indispensable by readers of Sheridan's time.

12 Philip Dormer Stanhope, 4th Earl of Chesterfield (1694–1773). His *Letters to His Son* advise prudent and sometimes highly artificial behaviour, guided by the lights of 'Reason' and 'knowledge of the world'. Romantic writers found the letters dangerously lacking in spontaneity and spiritual depth and attacked them as evidence of the limitation of the 'typical' eighteenth-century cast of mind.

13 The most celebrated and important English eighteenth-century novelist, Samuel Richardson (1689–1761) had a runaway success with *Pamela*, a journal novel written from the point of view of a socially ambitious fifteen-year-old girl. His masterpiece, *Clarissa* (1747–8) still has the distinction of being the longest novel in the language.

14 The cult of sensibility presented and analysed the highest human motives and behaviour, both in novels such as Henry Mackenzie's *The Man of Feeling* (1771) and plays such as Richard Cumberland's *The West Indian* (1771). Sheridan both satirizes and celebrates the form in his major comedies.

15 The Marquis de Sade (1740–1814) was a French aristocrat and libertine imprisoned for his 'sadistic' (his title is the origin of the word) behaviour and writings under every changing regime in France, including both the last Bourbon kings, the various revolutionary governments and Napoleon. His most famous literary work is *Justine: or the Misfortunes of Virtue* (1791).

A poem like Blake's 'The Clod and the Pebble' is not just a contribution to the canon of eighteenth-century eroticism[16]. It is part of the penetrating way Blake maps the human brain in *Songs of Innocence and of Experience*, and his mental voyage extends to as yet unknown territories well beyond the speculations of Samuel Richardson or Sheridan's Lydia Languish. For Blake, if 'the doors of perception'[17] were to be thoroughly cleansed (no more priests, no more tyrants, no more prudish or prudent hypocrisy), human potential and human speculations might stretch out without limits, across what Hamlet calls 'infinite space'[18]. Blake regularly complained that Bacon, or Locke, or Newton, or Sir Joshua Reynolds[19], or some other great figure of the Enlightenment, preferred to make prisons of their thoughts rather than set their speculations truly free, letting go the 'mind-forged manacles', enfranchising the 'chartered' streets (of 'London'). Throughout his life Blake returned to an image of God the Father that reflected this exasperation with contemporary science and theology alike. He calls God the Ancient of Days, not because of his biblical wisdom, but because he is past his sell-by date. Blake depicts him forgetting the beauty of his own body and the pulsing universe in favour of describing arbitrary boundaries with a pair of compasses, and writing it all down in a big rule book[20]. In the same way the Creator (the 'Holy Word') in the 'Introduction' to *Songs of Experience* seems to turn selfishly away from the world he has created. Blake didn't believe that eternity was marked up by timid gods into no-go areas, 'Thou shalt not!' written over the door ('The Garden of Love').

Thus both writers argue against system and reckoning. A similar distrust of self-imposed limits can be seen in their handling of literary models, and the literature of their own times. Blake's *Songs* are not modelled upon the Horatian satire[21] that had

---

16   In addition to the works of the Marquis de Sade, this is also the century of John Cleland's erotic best-seller *Fanny Hill* (1748–9) and the frequently obscene parodies of Richardson's *Pamela* (1740).

17   The phrase is from Blake's *Marriage of Heaven and Hell*, written at the same time as the conflated version of *Songs* (1794).

18   *Hamlet* Act 2, Scene 2, line 255.

19   Francis Bacon, Lord Verulam (1561–1626), early modern philosopher held at this time to be the father of modern science; John Locke (1632–1704), author of *An Essay Concerning Human Understanding*, philosopher who believed all knowledge comes not from inspiration but from our personal experience; Sir Isaac Newton (1643–1727), the most important and influential British scientist before Darwin; Sir Joshua Reynolds (1723–92), founder of the Royal Academy of Art and the most influential painter of Blake's formative years.

20   Blake's image of a white-bearded God measuring out his creation with a pair of compasses (see Proverbs 8:27) was a favourite of the artist's. He originally etched the design in 1794, the year of *Songs of Innocence and of Experience*. The 'Ancient of Days' is a Jewish name for God, as found in Daniel 7:9.

21   The ethical commitment of Quintus Horatius Flaccus (68 BCE –8 CE), satirist of the excesses of Augustus's reign but apologist for Augustus (63 BCE –14 CE), made him the most important literary model for eighteenth-century poets, especially Alexander Pope (1688–1744) who imitated nearly all his Satires and Epistles.

dominated the taste of the eighteenth century. Instead they reflect a contemporary appetite for lively narrative poems (oral ballads were collected and edited at this time)[22], combining this with the emotional charge of the Evangelical revival[23] (this was the great age of the hymn). Yet Blake's purpose remains as resolutely and efficiently satirical as any eighteenth-century poet. 'The *Songs of Experience* are satires,' wrote Northrop Frye[24], 'but one of the things that they satirise is the state of innocence… conversely the *Songs of Innocence* satirise the state of experience.' On the title page of *Songs of Innocence and of Experience* (1794) Blake suggests that the poems are meant to illustrate the 'Two Contrary States of the Human Soul' and, read together, the 'counterpart' poems become mutually challenged and informative to the point of incandescence. Sheridan's satirizing of human limitations and folly is cooler than Blake's, and also more obviously in keeping with the literary decorum of the eighteenth century, with its elegant rhythmic prose, and the neatness achieved by frequent resort to abstractions and antitheses:

> When hearts deserving happiness would unite their fortunes, virtue would crown them with an unfading garland of modest, hurtless flowers; but ill-judging passion will force the gaudier rose into the wreath, whose thorn offends them, when its leaves are dropped! (Act 5, Scene 3, lines 310–15)

To some extent Sheridan's tight and tidy expression fits the rather tame excesses he satirizes in the theme park of late eighteenth-century Bath: silly fire-eating non-duels, ladies on sofas reading prurient books about adultery, while they curl and stain the pages with dirty fingernails (the rather timid afternoons of 'Lady Slattern Lounger', Act 1, Scene 2, lines 15–21). Yet the dramatist, foreshadowing Blake, has also caught the progressive mood of literature in the 'Age of Revolution', and two of his satirical targets, Faulkland and Malaprop, like the victim-beneficiaries of the complex love-entanglements in Blake's *Songs*, anticipate modern fascination with psychological motivation and the fantastic 'other'.

The first of these figures, *The Rivals*' secondary hero, Faulkland, seemed 'a decided bore' to Victorian producers of the play. They were unsure whether Sheridan was satirizing or indulging the too-scrupulous scrupling of the sentimental tradition. In any case, they thought the results 'irremediably dated', and did what they could to

---

22 For instance, by Bishop Percy's *Reliques of Ancient English Poetry* (1765), Joseph Ritson's *Ancient Songs* (1792) and Sir Walter Scott's *Minstrelsy of the Scottish Border* (1802–3).

23 The Evangelical revival is a movement characterized by strong religious emotion usually held to be a reaction to the drabness or dryness of much eighteenth-century piety. Before 1800 it is strongest in the Methodist movement, but from the turn of the century, following a split with the Methodists, it became a strong and influential movement within the Established Church of England. Its valorizing of subjective religious experience gives it some similarities with Romanticism.

24 In the first major academic study of Blake, *Fearful Symmetry* (1947).

prune Faulkland's lines. But modern productions, aware that the cult of sensibility, among other things, is a forerunner of analyst's psychobabble, have found room for him again. The bizarre emotional logic by which in Act 5, Scene 1 he provokes Julia to rush exasperated from his presence purely out of a desire to spare her any pain is not far from the moral mantraps of Blake's 'The Clod and the Pebble'. One critic has suggested he should be played as a professional analyst's patient, obsessively raking over his emotions.

The second character to transcend her eighteenth-century origins is Mrs Malaprop. At first sight, her wrenching of vocabulary looks traditional: after all, there were Malaprops, Bottom and Dogberry[25] for instance, in Shakespeare's plays. However Mrs Malaprop is richer and stranger than this. She can be played by actresses of almost any age, who may choose to stress her insecurities, but who may choose instead to foreground her overweening self-confidence and self-projection, which is almost that of a performance artist. She re-writes the world (quite literally) with arias[26] of linguistic fantasy; her language, like that of Dickens's Mrs Gamp[27], operates in a sealed linguistic world, ultimately about and responsible only to itself. Top-notch Malaprop phrases such as the 'pineapple of politeness' (teased out from Jack's reference to an 'orange-tree', Act 3, Scene 3, lines 23–6) and 'a nice derangement of epitaphs' (line 79) seem close to the hard-core nonsense[28] of another Victorian, Edward Lear. But the glowing certainties of Mrs Malaprop's fantasy world of words, which mean more than the dictionary says, also resemble the robust and challenging alternative universes so many Romantic outsiders (beggars, slaves, children, chimney-sweeps) seem to carry around in their heads. When Blake's 'Chimney-Sweeper' goes laughing down an imaginary 'green plain' instead of facing up to his snow- and soot-bound sufferings, when his 'Little Vagabond' wants to make church more like a pub, or follow unearthly lights like 'The Little Boy Lost', they are in some ways little Mrs Malaprops, reconditioning the world on their terms, rather than merely enduring 'things as they are'.

For both Blake and Sheridan celebrate, in their different ways, artifice. Blake's life was dedicated to trapping and sharing the artist's moments of vision, ensuring the experience was not impeded or unfortunately sophisticated by the taste of

---

25 Bottom, the thespian weaver in *A Midsummer Night's Dream* (c. 1594); Dogberry, the self-important policeman in *Much Ado About Nothing* (c. 1598).

26 Her longer speeches are like the songs of an operatic singer.

27 The drunken private nurse in Dickens's *Martin Chuzzlewit* (1844), who devises an imaginary friend, Mrs Harris, to provide her with glowing references. It follows she must concoct a world for Mrs Harris to inhabit. 'Mrs Harris, who does not even exist,' writes Orwell, 'has more detail piled on to her than any three characters in an ordinary novel' ('Charles Dickens', 1940).

28 The nonsense tradition in Victorian literature began with Edward Lear's limericks, originally written in the 1830s, and was carried on with mock-heroic nonsense poems like Lear's 'The Dong with a Luminous Nose' and Carroll's *The Hunting of the Snark* (1876). The weightless, fantastic satire of Wilde's *The Importance of Being Earnest* is possibly related to it.

publishers and critics. This can make his work seem naïve in its downrightness, a world away from the one Sheridan wrote for and amused at Covent Garden and later Drury Lane; but Blake's determination to act as 'total artist' and 'self-publisher', distributing each uniquely coloured (and sometimes uniquely paginated) copy of *Songs* only to a favoured few – something like the Ancient Mariner who knows which Wedding Guest he must stop[29] – is also a vindication of the sacredness of artifice and the artistic process: a book of Blake's designs should be made available only to those who come without prejudice to think and listen. The reason there are so few extant copies of the composite *Songs* (just 24) is that Blake kept every aspect of the creative process in his own hands: even the inks with which his limited editions were printed were made by himself and his wife.

The audiences of the early performances of Sheridan's *The Rivals* were probably less select and selective than the patrons who walked out of Blake's lodgings with copies of *Songs*, but they also belonged to a world that prized the artifice of 'artificial comedy'. Sheridan's artifice, like Blake's, draws persistent attention to itself. Public life involved elaborate 'surfaces' of hair and clothes. Society ladies pretended to be shepherdesses; the 'quality' took the waters in flannel blankets and beribboned hats; fashionable gatherings meant donning cockades, periwigs, powder, pomatum and stylized skin blemishes. Even fashionable architecture was not quite what it seemed. In Bath, John Wood the elder's Circus (1754–68)[30] only presents its iconic neoclassical frontage to the world from one theatrical angle: behind, out of sight, the houses were completed in a bewildering number of styles, with roofs at different heights, and as few or many out-offices as the individual owners preferred. Everything in Sheridan's play walks on literary stilts, and belongs to a world of artifice, much as Blake's confident simplicity, both of word and design, is a device to highlight his aesthetic originality. Blake sometimes inks the image of the Little Black Boy in *Innocence* realistically black or brown, but also (to emphasize that the limits of reality are soon reached), white or pink. In the 1770s *The Rivals* would have been performed with the house lights up, the characters speaking something like sublime (and sublimely ordered) nonsense to the audience, Mrs Malaprop re-writing history with the self-assurance of a prototype Lady Bracknell[31]: 'we will not anticipate the past' (Act 4, Scene 2, line 173).

Though *The Rivals* and *Songs of Innocence* are written in different genres, cross-genre comparison is informative. Though written in prose, *The Rivals* is a Romantic

---

29 In Samuel Taylor Coleridge's Gothic fantasy poem of sin and atonement, 'The Rime of the Ancient Mariner' (1798).

30 The Bath Circus (from the Latin word for 'ring') is a circular space surrounded by large townhouses, each with a neoclassical façade.

31 The surreal social arbiter and overweening matriarch in Wilde's *The Importance of Being Earnest* (1895).

comedy, making much use of poetic effect. In Act 5, Scene 1 Lydia rises to a kind of poetic shorthand, hiccupping highlights from the fashionable poetry of sentiment, separated by gasping dashes. She believes a Romantic elopement, complete with rope-ladders and a four-in-hand carriage, is her due. Her January assignations in the 'freezing blast' in the garden are warmed very poetically by the 'glow' of 'mutual ardour', as in Keats's equally domestic fantasy, 'The Eve of St Agnes' (1819). There is the same hot-cold effect in the kinky love poems of Blake's *Songs of Experience*, such as 'Ah! Sunflower', 'The Sick Rose' or 'The Clod and the Pebble'. If Lydia's poetic love-making seems out to prove that 'opposition is true friendship' (*The Marriage of Heaven and Hell*), Mrs Malaprop's arias recondition the loftiest poetry into something like nonsense verse. Alligators become allegories, psychiatry becomes hydrostatics, and Hamlet's speech in quest of his father shudders from one sublime misrepresentation to another, until it stops off at 'A station, like Harry Mercury, new' (Act 4, Scene 2, line 17)[32]. The surrealism of Malaprop's language resembles the note of hallucinatory horror Blake introduces into his synaesthesic poem[33] 'London', in which we 'hear' the clank of 'mind-forged manacles', churches become draped in something like funeral palls, and 'sighs' turn to blood-stains. Blake provides a more serious, but equally 'nice derangement of epitaphs'.

As Sheridan's play makes considerable use of poetic techniques, so Blake's poetry is strongly dramatic. The *Songs* have their origin, after all, in folk music and hymn-singing, and Blake was prepared to sing them to tunes now lost. Some of his poems also possess formidable narrative drive (for example, 'A Poison Tree'), and in the composite volume the poems pair off in something like staged dialogues, one speaker reflecting the vision of humankind a moment before, the other a moment after the Fall, the 'Innocent' speaker content with affirmation, his fallen companion stirring up argument. In Blake's poems, the debate ramifies as it moves from one paired poem to the other; in drama, however, innocence must be focused more consistently in a single character, so Sheridan chooses Julia. Julia's healthy soul is subordinated to Faulkland's cranky inner life for much of the play, but in the last scene she wins out with a fragrant, flower-filled final speech, and speaks a vibrant epilogue. Early audiences were apparently enchanted with her, showing that, as in Blake, 'Innocence' is by no means invariably dull.

---

32 See *Hamlet* Act 3, Scene 4, lines 56–9:

> Hyperion's curls, the front of Jove himself,
> An eye like Mars to threaten and command,
> A station like the herald Mercury
> New-lighted on a heaven-kissing hill

33 Literary synaesthesia establishes a link between the perceptions of different senses. The most famous example is Orsino's description of the 'sweet sound' that 'breathes… Stealing and giving odour' (smell combined with hearing) 'upon a bank of violets' (*Twelfth Night* Act 1, Scene 1, lines 5–7).

The critical heritage of the two works shows intriguing variation. Sheridan's play appealed to his public much more rapidly and completely than Blake's poems. The latter made, as we've seen, little effort to share his designs with others unless they possessed appropriate imaginative sympathy. Sheridan's play, an overnight hit, has thus persistently raised the question from later critics as to whether it has sufficient depth to sustain itself as a canonical work. This is usually answered with a practical acknowledgement that no romantic comedy has held the stage better since Shakespeare, and none more continuously, for even Shakespeare was off the boards during the interregnum[34]. Blake's *Songs*, in his lifetime his only literary work that involved the cottage industry of himself and his wife in reprints, were at first shared with a small discerning audience, including Coleridge[35] and Charles Lamb[36], but their reputation spread steadily, aided by some weighty esteem from Wordsworth, the Poet Laureate[37]. A landmark biography from Alexander Gilchrist ensured Blake starred in the Victorian cult of all things Romantic, and by the 1860s his pre-eminence among the writers of short lyrics in English was assured.

The craftsmanship of each writer is widely admired, and the shared accessibility of both Sheridan's sophisticated play and Blake's slight but muscular songs has guaranteed both writers a formidable afterlife among the popular classics of English literature. Neither seems ponderously chained to a world of periwigs, religious revivals or philosophic treatises; both assert their significance as writers of current importance (though Blake is sometimes misrepresented by students as an honorary 'Victorian', as if his work were a campaign against industry and for proper legislation of factories). As we have seen, Blake and Sheridan engage in profitable debate with one another over many of the key contextual issues at the turn of the eighteenth century; sometimes they collude. At times they seem a universe apart, Blake envisioning London as the New Jerusalem, Sheridan as a decent manor for a 'Mick on the Make[38]'. At other times their art seems curiously cohesive, separated only by the accident of class: Blake, with his brushes, easels and printing press on the unfashionable, working man's side of the Strand, Sheridan with the gods across the road, among the theatres, looking towards Westminster.

---

34 The period of Puritan government in London (1649–60) during which time the theatres were closed.
35 Samuel Taylor Coleridge (1772–1834), Romantic poet, critic and theologian.
36 Charles Lamb (1775–1834), Romantic essayist.
37 William Wordsworth (1770–1850), most influential Romantic poet.
38 Roy Foster's phrase.

Further reading
Biography
For background to Blake see Peter Ackroyd, *Blake* (1995)
For comprehensive collections of Blake's designs visit www.blakearchive.org

For background to Sheridan see:
Madeleine Bingham, *Sheridan: The Track of a Comet* (1972)
Peter Thomson, *The Cambridge Introduction to English Theatre, 1660–1900* (2006)
Janet Todd's Sensibility: *An Introduction* (1986)

Critical studies
P.H. Davison, ed., *Sheridan: Comedies* (Macmillan Casebook, 1986)
David V. Erdman, *Blake: Prophet Against Empire* (1954)
Northrop Frye, *Fearful Symmetry: A Study of William Blake* (1947)
David W. Lindsay, *Songs of Innocence and Experience* (1989)
Diane Maybank, ed. *Richard Brinsley Sheridan: The Rivals*, Oxford Student Texts edition (2012)
Richard Willmott, ed., *William Blake: Songs of Innocence and of Experience*, Oxford Student Texts edition (2011)
Katharine Worth, *Sheridan and Goldsmith* (1992)

Power and Excess in *The Wife of Bath's Prologue and Tale* by Geoffrey Chaucer and *The Rivals* by Richard Brinsley Sheridan

David Cockburn

A comparison of two texts? Between a poem and a play? Not only that, but a comparison between two different genres, written four hundred years apart? It may seem like a difficult task, but it is achievable. Literature tends to be about the social contexts of our lives; about the depiction of ideas, issues and feelings; and sometimes, overarchingly, about the exploration of something universal concerning the human condition. Such themes are not restricted to any particular era. Both *The Wife of Bath's Prologue and Tale* and *The Rivals* deal with the themes of power and excess, relevant in the centuries in which they were written, and all others.

Literature is almost always, in some way, about the use and abuse of power. *The Wife of Bath's Prologue and Tale*, with its power-hungry and power-mongering speaker, has the idea at its very centre. Indeed, that a woman of her time not only survives five husbands, but survives them with power to add to their number, may not strike all readers as entirely estimable, yet is a real measure of her strength. The title of almost every one of Chaucer's other tales is a statement of the narrator's status or function in society: *The Knight's Tale, The Miller's Tale, The Pardoner's Tale, The Friar's Tale*, and so on. Nor are things any different for female narrators: *The Prioress's Tale* or *The Second Nun's Tale*. But in the case of *The Wife of Bath*, there is no mention of her status – unless the implication is that being the *Wife* is the woman's status or function in society. By highlighting the word *Wife* Chaucer is, perhaps, drawing the reader's attention to her role and significance, which, despite conventional expectations of wifely submissiveness at this time, turns out to be that of a highly manipulative, powerful woman. One of the characteristics of this particular wife, it appears, is her love of power over each husband, over men. Because Sheridan's *The Rivals* is a drama, focusing on the schemes and desires of many separate characters rather than a monologue radiating from a single voice, his work naturally represents the kinetic energy of many 'rivals' jostling for power.

One of the most palpable things Sheridan's pomaded and brocaded people fight about, and with, is their clothing, an indicator for them of social class, income, taste and image. In Chaucer's General Prologue, where the reader is introduced to the Wife of Bath, clothing is also significant. Mention is made of Alisoun's 'coverchiefs ful fyne' which 'weyeden ten pound' as well as 'Hir hosen' which 'weren of fyn scarlet reed' (lines 453–6). Such descriptions not only help present and reflect the woman's character, but the clothes also send out a signal to the other pilgrims. The 'coverchiefs ful fyne', along with the flamboyant scarlet colour, might suggest to any modern reader the convention of power dressing, where a woman draws attention to herself by dressing ostentatiously. The colour red not only symbolizes aspiration, it also suggests a woman in the ascendancy. Moreover to a medieval audience Alisoun's elaborate dress sense would suggest that she had no great concerns about sumptuary laws[1], which were meant to ensure that people's dress both indicated and limited their status. In matters of personal appearance, as in so many other ways, Alisoun is pushing the boundaries. In addition to this, her vibrant dress sense and awareness of its social impact may suggest professional involvement in the clothing trade. Living near Bath, she comes from an important centre for the medieval clothing industry.

Four hundred years later Sheridan also chooses Bath for a setting. The city no longer deals directly in stuffs and woollens but, having become a self-indulgent playground for the idle rich, it still affords plenty of opportunities for sartorial one-upmanship. When, at curtain-up, Fag reprimands the Coachman for wearing a wig: 'What the devil do you do with a *wig*, Thomas? None of the London whips[2] of any degree of ton wear *wigs* now' (Act 1, Scene 1, lines 87–9) his remark bristles with self-importance. At that point in the eighteenth century, wigs were going out of fashion, and Fag, power-monger that he is, wants the Coachman to know not only that the latter's outmoded wig represents an effort at ineffectual social betterment that would be laughed at in London, but that it also infallibly labels Bath as behind the times.

Wigs had been a marker of social boundaries since the early Restoration[3]. During the Stuart and early Hanoverian eras, wigs were elaborate and expensive – Allan Ramsay's portrait of George III[4] in his coronation robes shows him wearing a sophisticated, intricately woven wig. By the time this play was written, Fag has abandoned his wig because fashionable gentlemen had already done so. The Coachman, on the other hand, retains his head covering because for him it symbolizes his own hard-won status on the social ladder, as well as an indication of traditional, well-mannered ways. In both texts the details of dress signify to a modern audience, with a little research or imagination on their part, what they

---

1   Sumptuary laws were laws to govern behaviour, in this case relating to acceptable forms of dress. In late medieval England this became a means of identifying social classes and therefore reinforcing social hierarchies. As a prosperous member of the middle class, Alisoun could afford rich fabric but the kind of clothes she should and should not wear was set out in legislation in an attempt to prevent people of her social rank from upstaging the aristocrats. However such legislation was not rigorously enforced in Chaucer's time.

2   Coachmen.

3   The restoration of the monarchy with Charles II in 1660, following eleven years of republicanism known as the interregnum.

4   Allan Ramsay (1713–84), is famous for his paintings of George III, Queen Charlotte, David Hume and Alexander Boswell. George III was King of Great Britain and Ireland from 1760–1820.

would have suggested to the fashionistas of the time: that dress can reveal much about social positioning and individual aspirations. The symbolic significance of clothes was important for people living at the time Chaucer was writing, and for Sheridan's audience four hundred years later, and still is for people today.

But clothes can also suggest excess. Alisoun's dress not only reveals something about her intentions but is also excessive. The weight and quantity of the garments alone are an indication of excess. In Act 5, Scene 1 of *The Rivals*, Faulkland also makes use of excessive costume when entering Julia's dressing room. He enters *'muffled up in a riding-coat'*, his purpose to 'take a long farewell' of his beloved, pretending that he has been drawn into a quarrel and must 'fly this kingdom' (lines 6, 12). His ruse, like his costume, is elaborate and appears to be inspired by the kind of events he might have read about in an early Gothic novel[5].

Faulkland, whether he means it or not, always arranges his behaviour to test the strength of Julia's love and fidelity; his dress is excessive, matching his behaviour and language. He is 'bankrupt in gratitude', asking her what 'little compensation poor Faulkland can make you beside his solitary love?' (lines 32–6). The language of transaction suggests that for him everything is a kind of verbal negotiation or bargain, his real feelings (and he does seem to have some, somewhere) buried beneath the grandiloquent folds of his cloak, and beneath his habitually absurd and melodramatic dialogue.

Faulkland's characteristic introspection, self-analysis and self-regard emerge, if not from the cloak, then from the dialogue delivered from beneath its comforting disguise. He talks about his 'natural fretfulness' (lines 52–3) and how he is 'Cursed… with more imperfections than my fellow-wretches' (lines 123–4). He laments: 'O love! Tormentor! Fiend! – whose influence, like the moon's, acting on men of dull souls, makes idiots of them, but, meeting subtler spirits, betrays their course and urges sensibility to madness!' (lines 130–34). The apparel of sentimental lover arguably gives him confidence (where on other occasions he appears timid), and he expresses his super-scrupulous view of his own motivation more intricately here than elsewhere in the play. The theatrical disguise may even allow Faulkland to voice something of the developing Romantic tendency to scrutinize personal impressions and feelings not just for their own sake, but to give them priority over rational thinking, and to view them as potentially authoritative, even prophetic. The great rational philosopher David Hume[6] died about the time the play was first

---

5 Gothic novels often deal with horror or the supernatural, usually in settings such as castles, vaults, churchyards, or gloomy, foreboding places, where characters are dressed in dark, many-layered clothes. Horace Walpole's *The Castle of Otranto* (1764) is considered to be one of the first Gothic novels.

6 David Hume (1711–76), was an Enlightenment philosopher and a rationalist with a strong interest in human motivation.

performed; Jean-Jacques Rousseau's[7] influential pre-Romantic writings were largely complete, and published; while Robert Burns[8], arguably the first great Romantic writer, was just sixteen, yet already writing his schoolboy poetry about love and feelings. The play was written on the cusp of the Age of the Romantics, and there is a way of viewing Faulkland (albeit depending on heavy, even ridiculous disguise) as an early, inchoate Romantic figure, certainly someone not only aware of his feelings but able to subject them to some psychological scrutiny.

Alisoun's power-dressing is much more overt than Faulkland's occasional use of dramatic costume. For Alisoun, everything is combative, as befits a character who argues like a battering-ram, and has more justifications to support her case than a defending barrister. Her Sunday veils weigh as much as some medieval breastplates, and her head, 'Ywympled wel' (General Prologue, line 470), recalls the new plate armour[9] of the time. Her hat is explicitly compared to a shield, she has 'a paire of spores sharpe' on her feet (line 473) and the Ellesmere manuscript illustration[10] shows her with a whip. Look out, her appearance proclaims, as she weighs into debate as if to do battle; look out you over-confident male chauvinists, Jerome, St Paul and – most of all – Jankyn! All this is very full-on, while Faulkland's muffled uncertainties suggest that this aspect of his persona remains in development.

If clothing reveals clues about the psychology it covers, then what the characters 'read' and how they refer to their 'reading' is equally meaningful. It is interesting that the very first word of *The Wife of Bath's Prologue* is 'Experience', which, she claims, 'is right ynogh for me/To speke of wo that is in mariage'. She claims she does not need the 'auctoritee' of the written text that was generally used to underpin opinion and even prejudice at this time (lines 1–3). The authorities she cites build up an unfavourable, misogynistic view of women. Male churchmen, such as St Jerome (line 674), Walter Map (line 671) and Eustache Deschamps all censure female sexuality, as does that well-known 'mayde' (line 79) Saint Paul, who conceded that wedlock was an acceptable second best to celibacy, but only if the alternative was damnation: 'Bet is to be wedded than to brynne' (line 52).

If Alisoun takes a dim view of the gender politics of schoolmen, the moral guardians in Sheridan's play are damned from their own mouths. Sir Anthony blames Lydia's obstinacy on her having been taught to read, while Mrs Malaprop, in a speech riddled

---

7   Jean-Jacques Rousseau (1712–78), believed that primitive man was preferable to civilized man; that knowledge had only served to corrupt human beings, and that, consequently, the child's imagination (and the need to shape and control it) should be at the heart of any educational system.

8   Robert Burns (1759–96), although an Enlightenment figure, was also an early Romantic poet.

9   Plate armour was a type of bespoke armour made of plates of steel or iron, worn in the fourteenth and fifteenth centuries.

10 The Ellesmere Chaucer, or Ellesmere Manuscript, is an early fifteenth-century illustrated manuscript of *The Canterbury Tales*. Colour illustrations include Chaucer himself, and the Wife of Bath on horseback, clutching a whip.

with mistaken words, lists the subjects that a young girl ought never to be taught, with the exception of 'geometry, that she might know something of the contagious countries' (Act 1, Scene 2, lines 262–3). She also believes that a girl 'at nine years old' ought to be sent to boarding school 'in order to learn a little ingenuity and artifice' (lines 258–9).

The irony of Mrs Malaprop's speech isn't lost on the audience. She wants to deny young girls an education while both displaying her own lack of linguistic expertise and continuing to make inappropriate assertions via her mistaken phrases. As Julia says, the fact that Mrs Malaprop's words are 'so ingeniously misapplied, without being mispronounced' (Act 1, Scene 2, lines 161–2) shows that, despite Malaprop's law-making, her actual meaning is perpetually undermined by her intellectual vacuity.

Adding to the irony, Sir Anthony supports Mrs Malaprop's received ideas about the parenting of daughters: he avers that 'Had I a thousand daughters, by heaven, I'd as soon have them taught the black art as their alphabet' (Act 1, Scene 2, lines 229–30). Better to curb female wishes, especially concerning marriage, by using parental power to 'enforce this matter roundly': if Lydia rejects his proposal then Mrs Malaprop must 'clap her under lock and key' (lines 301–3), starving her if need be. Such excessive language seems to satirize itself, suggesting that, like Alisoun's biblical commentators, these self-appointed moral sentinels are ripe for contradiction.

Alisoun turns out to be adept at deconstructing biblical texts so that a libertarian meaning shines forth. She quotes the Book of Revelation[11] when she states that 'Virginitee is greet perfeccion' (line 105), but she also makes a quick assessment that this is intended for those 'that wolde lyve parfitly', making it clear to her listeners that she does not abide by it: 'lordynges, by youre leve, that am nat I' (lines 111–2). Virginity is not for Alisoun; she prefers the physicality of sex. But more than that: she tells her husbands that 'al is for to selle', and as long as she can profit from the transaction of marriage – empowering herself, as it were, with each man's wealth – she is willing to allow him some concessions. For instance, she 'wolde… al his lust endure', while she made 'a feyned appetit' to enjoy the business of love-making, even though 'in bacon', her metaphor for ageing bodies, 'hadde I nevere delit' (lines 414–8). Thus Alisoun gains power over men by making free use (or misuse) of her sexuality, as well as making reference to other texts, many of which are misconstrued, misapplied or presented with frank insolence. In the tale itself,

---

11 The Book of Revelation is the final book of the New Testament, in which the author describes apocalyptic visions, though scholars claim these are open to any number of interpretations.

for example, she makes reference to Midas's wife in Ovid's *Metamorphoses*[12], but she alters Ovid's narrative to make Midas reveal his secret to his wife (and not his barber), thus supporting her contention that women cannot keep secrets ('we kan no conseil hyde') and to argue that there is no point in men encouraging them to do so.

The Wife's driving need to show that women are incontrovertible forces of nature is also perhaps emphasized by the brevity of the tale she tells. She has so much to say of her use and pursuit of power over men that her narrative becomes little more than reinforcement of her familiar views. In the tale she tells of a reformed rapist. Through the presentation of this character, she suggests that, contrary to attitudes towards women of the day, it is the male who indulges in matters of the flesh, while the old woman is presented as sensible and thoughtful. Although the knight demonstrates physical power, he is nevertheless presented as a victim of his own sexuality, feeble-minded, naive and weak. At each stage of the tale it is the women who decide the knight's fate – the queen, the hag – and even the task the hero is given is a measure of the power of women, since the knight has to find out what women most desire. The answer, in keeping with the Wife's philosophy, is 'maistrie', power over the husband in marriage, an idea already amply rehearsed in Alisoun's outspoken Prologue. Thus she reduces her tale, where the characters must inevitably take over from her own self-advertising persona, to a side-show. The tale makes up just 32% of the total text, whereas in other prologues and tales the proportion of the tale is much larger: for example, *The Franklin's Tale* forms 94% and in the *Prioress's Prologue and Tale*, the tale forms 79% of the whole. Thus, as so often, Alisoun tailors a literary original – in this case a folk-tale – to suit her own egocentric needs.

If the Wife is adept at manipulating a small variety of texts – fairy tales, scripture and the classics – for rhetorical purposes, Lydia Languish, in *The Rivals*, appears to have a much greater literary collection on which to draw. When we meet her, in the second scene of *The Rivals*, it is in the context of the small travelling library she has accumulated (some twenty books are named). For both Lydia and Alisoun, reading, and making use of that reading, is thus a source of sometimes transgressive and always transformative power. Chaucer may be using the excessive claims of his male authorities to mock the Church and churchmen because they often interpret the Bible for their own ends or to support spurious arguments. Lydia may herself make 'creative' use of scripture by concealing her unorthodox reading by including

---

12 Ovid (Publius Ovidius Naso) wrote *Metamorphoses*, a Latin narrative poem of fifteen books, at the beginning of the first century. Among other tales, Ovid tells of how King Midas is punished by Apollo for voting against him in a music contest, by being given a pair of donkey's ears. Ashamed, Midas tries to hide his ears under his head garments. In Ovid's version of the story, Midas is then betrayed by his barber who, unable to keep the secret any longer, digs a hole in the ground and whispers into it. Later a patch of reeds grows on the spot and whispers Midas's secret for everyone to hear.

modern sermons and commentaries in her library[13]. For instance, she has a copy of the Protestant devotional manual *The Whole Duty of Man* (lines 30, 171), and a set of 'Fordyce's *Sermons*' (line 175), which emphasized the importance of 'elegance' and 'delicacy', and were written for the especial use of 'Young Women'. Both Alisoun and Lydia are very much aware of the bullying sub-text that was often enfolded within the patriarchal discourse of their times, and each, in her own way, is able to use it creatively to somehow facilitate her own ends.

In addition to sermons and conduct-books, which we assume Lydia will use pragmatically rather than in the spirit of piety, she has eighteenth-century classics by Smollett, Sterne, Mackenzie and Lord Chesterfield[14], together with texts such as Treyssac de Vergy's *The Mistakes of the Heart* and Paul Scarron's *The Innocent Adultery*, both of which would have been regarded at the time as unsuitable reading for a lady. One reviewer described Treyssac de Vergy's work as 'too luxuriant for the eye of delicacy', while George H. Nettleton described the latter title as 'a thoroughly indecent romance'. Therefore, while not an 'expert in al myn age' as is Alisoun (line 174), we can be sure that Lydia is well-read in the subject matter of life and love. This is partly what enables her to twist Jack Absolute round her little finger. Lydia leads him to entertain the prospect of a sentimental elopement; encourages him to kneel in the snow in a freezing January garden to do her homage (Act 5, Scene 1, lines 180–84); and, most significantly, to pretend to be an Ensign rather than a Captain because she prefers, and trusts, impecunious lovers.

Many of Alisoun's references seem to originate from that extraordinary bound volume of selected anti-feminist texts which her fifth husband, Young Jankyn, carries around with him obsessively, and which he seems, with obvious point, to have given the title 'book of wikked wyves' (line 685). The tome, and its contents, provide the battleground for the inter-generational couple (he was 'twenty wynter oold' and she was 'fourty', lines 600–601), but we note she does not insist on its being burnt before she has committed to memory choice details about its depiction of brutal, devious and insulting wives (Alisoun contributes her own insult about 'oold' men who are less use than an 'olde sho' in bed, lines 707–8).

When Alisoun is beaten by Jankyn it is because she tears three pages from his

---

13 The twenty works named in Act 1 of *The Rivals* were analysed in an article by George H. Nettleton, 'The Books of Lydia Languish's Circulating Library', *Journal of English and German Philology* 5 (1903–5), pp. 492–500. This is reprinted in *Sheridan: Comedies, A Casebook*, edited by Peter Davison (1986).

14 Tobias Smollett's *Humphry Clinker* (1771), named in *The Rivals*, is an eighteenth-century 'novel-in-letters'; Laurence Sterne, author of the quirky *Tristram Shandy*, would be better known to Lydia at this time as the writer of *A Sentimental Journey through France and Italy* (1768); Henry Mackenzie's *The Man of Feeling* (1771) is possibly the archetypal sentimental novel in English; while *The Letters of Lord Chesterfield* (1774) were written by the 4th Earl of Chesterfield, Philip Dormer Stanhope, to his unruly son. All four works would have been new in 1775, illustrating Lydia's modish taste in reading; and all may be construed in some way or other as conduct books.

precious book, in final exasperation over its sordid misogyny and self-justification. The subsequent fight is as farcical as it is perilous, but Alisoun eventually wins and gains dominance over him. The book's destruction almost acts as a symbolic seal, marking the end of his reign of authority over her; Alisoun gets 'By maistrie, al the soveraynetee' (line 818). She ends with the significant sentence, 'After that day we hadden never debaat' (line 822). It is intriguing how closely this episode of marital combat and symbolic book-burning mirrors the story the Wife goes on to tell of a lusty young man who considers himself lord of creation – and even commits rape – before being re-educated by a mature lady who, as a sort of moral by-product, is made young again by virtue of her wisdom and knowledge.

The Wife is so determinedly a driving force that she manages to subdue Jankyn with great cunning, while also doing her best to encourage the other pilgrims to accept her point of view. Lydia is much younger than Alisoun, and the late eighteenth-century society she inhabits is measured by a greater intricacy of social rules and expectations, especially those of taste and fashion. Her situation is thus less obviously 'free' than the situation that Alisoun has managed to win for herself. Lydia is fenced in by the patriarchal prejudices of other characters: the sway of Sir Anthony, the folly of Mrs Malaprop, and the determination with which the old try to direct the lives of the young.

Everything in Lydia's society is governed by protocol. There are protocols about how wards and their guardians should behave to each other, about conduct between fathers and sons, and protocols regarding marriage and arranged marriages. To circumvent these obstacles, characters serve time while employing tactics of deception, the excesses of which contribute much to the satirical energy of Sheridan's play. Even the serving girl Lucy, in her soliloquy at the end of Act 1, reveals her determination to benefit from the dissembling of her 'betters'. She keeps an account, costing the services she has performed, thus revealing through her cunning the power she has to charge them for their deceptive behaviour. Sheridan's depiction of Bath society is one where there seem to be opportunities at all levels to outwit and outmanoeuvre others. Lucy is no 'simpleton', but a cleverly manipulative woman, determined to climb the social ladder.

By the end of the play both Faulkland and Lydia succeed in securing the loves and the lovers they want. Julia tells Faulkland that she is one 'who would have followed you in beggary through the world!' (Act 5, Scene 1, lines 119–20). In her advice to Lydia, distraught at finding out that Beverley is, in fact, Jack Absolute, Julia counsels that she should not 'let a man, who loves you with sincerity, suffer that unhappiness from your *caprice*' (lines 192–3); Julia is thinking not only of Lydia's situation, but also of her own.

Both of these young women ultimately prove that love is empowered not as a result of mere 'caprice', but through an understanding of human nature. It is not only a matter of clever manipulation and sentimental indulgence, but having also the sensitivity to know how and when to sympathize with and reward their partners. This ultimately becomes the driving force of the marital careers on which they embark at the final curtain.

Neither *The Wife of Bath's Prologue and Tale* nor *The Rivals* is unique in exploring the topic of power, or indeed excesses that arise in pursuit of power. What both do extremely well, however, despite the four hundred years that separate them, is to show how readily people can gain authority from the ways in which they present or re-present themselves, whether this is achieved through the clothing they wear or the ways in which they 'interpret' the authorities that confine them. Moreover, in both texts, these means provide an opportunity by which women might redress the imbalance of power within their relationships as well as the immediate space they inhabit within their quite separate patriarchal societies.

Further reading
Critical studies
Steven Croft, ed., *Geoffrey Chaucer: The Wife of Bath's Tale*, Oxford Student Texts edition (2007)
Peter Davison, ed., *Sheridan: Comedies, A Casebook* (1986)
Diane Maybank, ed., *Richard Brinsley Sheridan: The Rivals*, Oxford Student Texts edition (2012)

Approaching the Assessment

The following section provides tips and advice about how to read and study your texts, as well as how to approach the assessment.

Context and comparison

In Section B of paper F663, with its combination of pre-1800 drama and poetry, you need to be able to show that you have an overall understanding of context, that is, the historical and literary worlds from which your texts emerged. If your texts are close in terms of the dates when they were written, you may be dealing with only one overarching context; if they are from different periods, you may be looking at context comparatively – considering the differing influences that produced each work.

You will also need to become sensitive to 'echoes' or parallels across your two texts, for example scenes, situations or moments with similar or related effects.

The Shakespeare text you have studied for Section A of the paper may help you to explore the context of drama including its concerns, characteristics and effects.

Spotting links and contrasts

When studying and writing about the texts, don't try to compare all the time: it is important that you get to know **each text in its own right**.

You are likely to spot overlapping concerns in the texts as you start to read the second one. If you are studying in a group, share your ideas and discuss them with your teacher and your fellow students.

Be innovative in your thinking: the best answers examiners see are often fresh and original – so you may be the first person to make the connection you have just spotted. Your teacher certainly won't have a set of 'right answers' – this paper is about exploration and discovery.

The shape of the question

In the exam, you will be presented with six questions and you must decide which of the six tasks to respond to. You should consider which task is likely to lead to the most relevant and interesting discussion of your texts.

All the questions on the paper begin with a proposition, in quotation marks. This quotation is designed to help you to focus and sharpen your thoughts. If you ignore it, your answer is likely to be very vague, and therefore weaker than if you set out to respond to the quotation in your argument.

It is important to read the entire question before you begin your answer. The best answers respond to the whole quotation, rather than just the first part of it. Often the final words in these quotations offer the most specific, and therefore most intriguing, angles for exploration.

In your answer, you don't have to reach an absolute conclusion – examiners want you to play with ideas. If the question does lead you to a conclusion, however, that's good, as it will suggest that your exploration of the texts has led you to a discovery.

Writing your answer

Examiners expect, in this paper, to see answers forming themselves as they are written: this is to be expected, given the unseen nature of the questions and the time constraints within which you are working.

When you begin your answer, however, you should show the examiner where you are going. Even when you do not know where, in the larger scheme, your argument may be heading, it helps to set out a sense of your initial ideas (with mention of both texts) in your opening paragraphs.

This does not mean writing a long introduction, commencing: 'In this essay I am going to write about…' You should begin your argument straight away. However, it is beneficial to show the examiner that you have a direction in mind. Of course, you won't know what your conclusion is going to be because you will be making up your mind as you write; what you offer in your opening paragraph will be a sorting-out, in general terms, of the essay's ingredients, like assembling the ingredients for a recipe before you cook.

Keeping both texts in play

Do not get stuck in one text! The most successful answers show frequent movement between the two texts – sometimes detailed examination of the two together, but often simply thoughtful asides ('as shown more obviously by Satan's exaggeration'; 'unlike Chaucer's more outspoken character'). To write exclusively about one text at length before writing about the other text is a much riskier approach, giving less opportunity for comparison and contrast. However, you don't have to mention both texts in every paragraph.

Referring to context

Not all candidates seem to realize the importance of context in this assessment, but it is vital. You need to show how the world of ideas and historical events influenced the creation of each text. In particular, you need to be aware that your authors had a philosophy of writing, and may well have formally written down their theories.

If your text reflects big ideas of the period – ideas such as heroism, the epic, comedy, tragedy, hubris – you need to be sure you know what these terms mean. Similarly, if you are studying a text that deals with religion, you need to understand the background. You should try to immerse yourself in the mental and cultural worlds of your two texts, and consider how they reflect the issues and attitudes of their times.

Using evidence to support your ideas

Really good answers make use of telling details or short quotations to support the argument and the comparisons. This method of selecting and presenting evidence from the texts helps to establish a sense of intelligent confidence; if you can link details across the texts, it shows real command of the materials.

Final points

Make sure you know your texts really well. Read them and let them work on your imagination. Put them on an MP3 player and listen to them. Read around them – for example, other authors from a similar period, historical texts. Don't wait for your teachers to find things. Try to be the leader of your own explorations. There are some very good critical anthologies available, for example, which are certainly worth looking at.

In preparation for your exam, grab the chance to write against the clock. This is vital practice for the exam. Cross-mark answers with your fellow students and exchange ideas.

Think hard when you see a question. Ask yourself, 'what is the quotation really getting at?'. Make brief notes on the page before you begin to write. Remember: to ignore the quotation is to miss the heart of the question.

When you write your answer, remember to say what you really think – and give evidence for your views.

Sample Student Response 1

The following sample answer is a high-band response to Unit F663 Section B. This response is based on *'Tis Pity She's a Whore* by John Ford and *The Wife of Bath's Prologue and Tale* by Geoffrey Chaucer. The footnotes provide feedback on the response and the answer is also followed by a summative comment on page 70, which summarizes its strengths and weaknesses.

'Desire is a kind of madness.' In the light of this view, discuss ways in which writers explore desire. In your answer, compare one drama text with one poetry text.

Both John Ford and Geoffrey Chaucer represent desire through their texts' themes of religious morality and right versus wrong, and the idea of what it actually is to be human in a world of temptation.[1]

In Ford's *'Tis Pity She's a Whore*[2] the lead character Giovanni's desire to be a Renaissance man, with new-found humanist knowledge, is clear. Evidence of his aspiration and desire comes from the play's opening scene. Meeting his confessor, Bonaventura, Giovanni says: 'To you I have unclasped my burdened soul... Must I not do what all men else may – love?'[3] His desire is clear, yet the view that 'desire is a kind of madness' appears clear too.[4] Some critics have suggested that in disobeying his 'ghostly father' Giovanni is challenging the Catholic establishment that dictates so much of what happens in the play.[5] Others feel his speech connotes his arrogance. Giovanni's arrogance and hubris, if not his madness, are indicated by his hatred of the 'customary form' that stops him sleeping with his sister. His desire demands that there should be no 'bar... 'twixt my perpetual happiness and me'. This suggests that Giovanni is stuck between two time zones and two belief systems in the late Elizabethan/early Renaissance era, not long after Elizabeth I converted England from a Catholic country to a Protestant one. It may be interpreted that Ford uses the character of Giovanni to connote the struggle between traditional Catholic religious beliefs and new-found humanism in the Renaissance era. His self-confidence may also reflect the arrogance of young Royalists in the years leading to the Civil War.[6] This would suggest why some have labelled Giovanni a tragic hero, displaying the inner struggle of a man caught between traditional Catholic, now Protestant beliefs, and new Renaissance beliefs. Thus his desire to challenge the moral limits of his age is one of the most intriguing struggles seen throughout *'Tis Pity She's a Whore*.[7]

---

1   AO1 The texts are introduced and linked by clear address to one central proposition in the quotation: desire.
2   AO1 Direct address to one text, placing it in an overall AO4 context.
3   AO2 Brisk textual substantiation of AO1/4 point.
4   AO2 Develops argument to include question's second term: madness.
5   AO3 Relevant awareness of critical debate.
6   AO4 Partially developed (if rather rushed and cryptic); reference to AO4 cultural context.
7   AO4 Provides an overall sense of the text in its context, with implied relevance to the question. Text 1 fully introduced.

Differing from *'Tis Pity*, in Chaucer's *The Wife of Bath's Prologue and Tale* the main character's desire has been interpreted as less of a radical statement, more as a reflection of her sex life.[8] The Wife tells of how she will have what she wants, and justifies her desires with reference to scripture, literature and her own experience. Some historicist critics have suggested that Chaucer uses his main character to criticize the Catholic Church and especially its complacent male defenders. This is made apparent through Chaucer's representation of the Wife's desires through the character of the Wife, especially through her desires for social betterment, esteem and 'maistrie', all of which are traditionally opposed in the Church's attitude to women. Evidence of this comes in the lines where the Wife says she is 'expert in al myn age' on the troubles of marriage. She attacks famous anti-feminists like St Paul and St Jerome, calling them 'olde kaynard' (dotard) or 'Sire olde fool', and arguing with them point by point, often taking what they say out of context. This would suggest that, differing from Giovanni, the Wife's desires are not caused by the need to pass the limits placed upon her by society, but a desire that is simply for the character's own selfish needs. As she says in the 'prayer' at the end of her tale: 'Jhesu Crist us sende / Housbondes meeke, yonge, and fressh abedde'. This may be the reason why Giovanni has been called a tragic hero and the Wife is viewed as struggling for her own social position and 'maistrie' in marriage.[9]

However, in comparing the two texts, it would appear that some of these ideas are similar and contributed to the making of the texts as they were when first written, either in the Caroline Era or the medieval era.[10] This contemporary style has been suggested to come from the texts' vision of desire and what it actually is to be human in a world of temptation. *The Wife of Bath's Tale* today has been interpreted as Chaucer showing the desires of an early feminist heroine, confronting entrenched masculine forces in her era. However, in the medieval era it was commonly believed that the fewer materialistic goods you had, the closer relationship you would have with God. So it would also appear that, although the Wife uses her sexual favours to fulfil her desires, making her husbands 'swynke' in bed to madness, her initial true desire, unchanged since she was a girl, 'flour', not 'bren', is to become part of a fairy-tale world of romance such as she presents in her tale, and to live in it. This desire may be classed as escapist, but is not really 'a kind of madness'. Her desires have brought her a kind of fulfilment, as she says, she has had her 'world as in my tyme'. Thus her needs have done no harm, but the cloud of a corrupt medieval society and its male cruelty, for example the unruly behaviour of the knight in her tale,

---

8   AO3 Comparison and differences between texts 1 and 2 help to establish a reading of Chaucer's text, with reference to context (AO4) and other critical views (AO3). AO2 references are fluently used to substantiate points.

9   AO3 Reinforces the contrast between the texts at the end of the initial discussion of text 1 (which is rather compressed). Both texts are now in play.

10 Paragraph focuses on desire in Chaucer's text but the wording is slightly unclear. Provides evidence (AO2) and discusses critical views with confidence (AO3). Discusses whether Wife's desire is 'madness'.

have overshadowed them. Thus it is the changing times, religion and society that morph the character of the Wife. Therefore, perhaps Chaucer connotes these ideas to show that human desire is imperfect and temptation can sometimes overcloud the moral duty to follow God's teachings. [11]

This idea is continued in Ford's *'Tis Pity*, particularly the idea of a world full of social and sexual temptation, and the idea that humans, haunted by desire, find it hard to remain on the straight path. [12] These ideas are seen throughout *'Tis Pity*, and it may be argued that the final scene of the play, a bloodbath that typifies the genre of revenge tragedy, sums up these ideas. In the last scene, Florio calls Giovanni 'a frantic madman', an emblem of the madness and horror that consume the desires of love in the play's final moments. The Cardinal blames everybody for failing to control their desires, then confiscates their ill-gotten gains 'to the Pope's proper use', a connotation from Ford that his hypocritical actions show what it actually is to be human in a tarnished world of mixed motives as well as desires. This mixture of double motives, of ideals with corruption, is shown in the play's use of heart imagery. An actual disembodied heart has been used to represent the seat of desire, temptation and human love throughout time in plays, poems and prose. It has been suggested that the references to Laura's heart in Petrarch's sonnets show the poet often wishes to possess or even dissect the seat of his love for Laura, her heart. Ford's play, in having Giovanni dig in the 'rich mine' of his beloved's body to extract her heart and hold it on the point of his sword for all to see, makes literal what in most Renaissance love stories remains just a symbol of desire. Thus Ford in *'Tis Pity* uses the disembodied heart to represent the homicidal desires of Parma society and their tainted outcomes. In some productions Giovanni is shown as having been driven quite mad by these bloodthirsty desires. On the other hand in *The Wife of Bath's Tale*, Alisoun does not tear out the hearts of her lovers, but 'tikled' them fondly, and her own heart's 'roote' is also 'tikled' by the memories she has built up of her varied and considerable experience. This different use of heart imagery in the two works may make it clear that the Wife's desires are not selfish and self-seeking, like Giovanni's, ending in a bloodbath, but sane, generous and give-and-take, though they do sometimes lead her into dubious acts.

In conclusion, the view that 'desire is a kind of madness' appears true, in a sense. [13] The initial ideas in both Ford's *'Tis Pity She's a Whore* and Chaucer's *The Wife of Bath's Prologue and Tale* appear to show the limits, even the dangers of human desires when

---

11 AO1 Points are valid but are too compressed producing a rather cryptic density of argument. The religious aspect of the argument is perhaps slightly distracting from the main point.

12 This paragraph looks at desire in *'Tis Pity*, by contrast and uses AO2 detail of the 'heart' imagery and dramatic action to reveal the extreme nature of desire in Ford's text, with reference to Giovanni's madness. A clever use of 'heart' references establishes a comparative link with Chaucer's text and leads to the final paragraph.

13 AO1 The conclusion shows the contrast between the extremes of Ford's play and the more humane and understandable motivations of the Wife, thus evaluating 'madness'. However, the wording could be clearer.

put against themes of religion and right versus wrong. However, the in-depth detail and connotations of characters whose society, arguably, challenges and restrains their desires, would suggest that humans may be driven to bloody madness by desire, as happens to Giovanni, Annabella, and the collection of whores, adulterers, double-crossers and gold-diggers in Ford's play; but it is also possible, as the Wife shows, to live in harmony with one's needs. Their desires show the complex nature of them, as seen particularly through Giovanni, Annabella and the cruel revenger Vasques, but also, the Wife.

This essay clearly reaches the top band – it is thoughtful, well informed and well illustrated; it handles the texts comparatively with skill, and it shows a clear grasp of the contrasting contexts, concerns and methods of the two texts. The characteristics of each text – the Wife's directness and the extreme nature of Ford's material – help to define the other. Clarity is less secure: the conclusion, in particular, could be more incisive and linked more clearly to the quotation in the question. The essay demonstrates that desire is disruptive, but that while it can lead to madness, it can also lead to fulfilment. It is a pity that the conclusion does not state this more clearly. The answer is likely to be at the lower–mid end of the top band.

Sample Student Response 2

The following sample answer is a middle-band response to Unit F663 Section B. This response is based on *'Tis Pity She's a Whore* by John Ford and *The Wife of Bath's Prologue and Tale* by Geoffrey Chaucer. The footnotes provide feedback on the response and the answer is also followed by a summative comment on page 73, which summarizes its strengths and weaknesses.

> **'Desire is a kind of madness.' In the light of this view, discuss ways in which writers explore desire. In your answer, compare one drama text with one poetry text.**

Both the lovers in *'Tis Pity* and the Wife have moments of madness.[1] The characters of both works lived in times where religion was a definitive part of society (although *'Tis Pity* is put in a time where everything was being questioned).[2] The two characters go against possibly the most powerful force in many ways and continue to do it even though the pleasures they seek can't save them.[3]

All these characters as soon as we encounter them are fully formed.[4] In *'Tis Pity*, where the powerful Cardinal and therefore the Catholic Church is watching, the characters continue to have sex, while the Wife only talks about the sex she has had. She states what she has accomplished and what she intends to capture next with the power of her bele chose or quoniam. Giovanni and Annabella go back to their incest even after she seems to have repented committing it.[5]

Everyone seems already to have set their minds to go against the will of God. The Wife has done so for pleasure and independence whereas Giovanni and Annabella do so because they are 'star-crossed lovers' and cannot help it. The other citizens of Parma behave like whores because they are in a city where everyone does so.[6]

Giovanni is, from his first appearance with the Friar, a man who does not like to govern his desire and does not see why he should do so. He is very much a Renaissance man, questioning everything and aiming for the highest level of achievement in every field he can,[7] a far cry from the well-behaved young man Romeo is in *Romeo and Juliet*, which Ford often quotes from in his play.[8] Chaucer does not represent the Wife as an

---

1   AO1 The essay jumps straight into identifying madness as a focus (though this is only one term in the question).
2   Very generalized AO4 statement.
3   AO1 It's not entirely clear how this reference to religion addresses the question.
4   Cryptic comment seems to relate to a theory of characterization which is not explained.
5   Ambitiously, the candidate talks about both texts in a paragraph about sex, incorporating AO2 quotations (not in quotation marks). This paragraph apparently talks about the 'pleasures' mentioned in paragraph 1.
6   This is lively, but very generalized. The reference to *Romeo and Juliet* is interesting, but not explained.
7   It would be helpful to have some AO2 detail here.
8   A fuller reference to *Romeo and Juliet*.

evil woman nor as a good-doer; there is no black or white with her. Alisoun falls in the grey zone, whereas in contrast Ford paints Giovanni as an outright rebel, whose desire causes him to cruelly tear out his sister's heart and mount it on his sword. He does not behave like a 'kind' relation to Annabella, who says 'unkind, unkind' to him at the end of the play. He is immediately shown as a man who disobeys the Bible: 'Cursed be he that lieth with his sister.'

Chaucer shows the Wife as a look-before-you-leap character who without really thinking does what she wants[9] and almost immediately becomes a slave to her passions even though she likes to believe she's in power.[10]

Giovanni rejects the Friar's arguments because it suits him to do so, and Soranzo is always making threats as to what God will step in and do if people do not obey him. Chaucer paints the Wife as a character who is not honest about her motives, but always finds reasons to support herself. She is very confident and also tells us how dangerous friars can be, preferring to make up her own mind. She thinks so well of these desires she looks at Jankyn's legs when she ought to concentrate on burying her previous husband.[11]

Although Giovanni swears love to his sister some critics think he is like Marlowe's Faustus, 'dabbling in a selfish love' for his own ends. In this we clearly see he is a Renaissance man on a quest for power, and it spices him that he can cross a forbidden boundary when he makes love to his sister. He insists his fate drives him on to the bloody tragedy of the conclusion but it is more likely his own dastardly desire.

Now whereas Giovanni thinks himself a 'fiery particle' experimenting with right and wrong, the Wife never questions what she's doing. She knows she's going to offend male writers with her desires and it pleases her. For her desire is the same as 'maistrie'. She twists the books she has read and often quotes bits out of context, boasting about the sinful acts she has done. This side of the Wife is explored in the prologue deeply enough that you're able to connect to her.

Even through Alisoun's lies and fraudulence we see that she is honest about her desires. These aspects of her personality blend well with her loud, overdressed appearance where it's hard to tell exactly how rich she is (as at this time you usually could), much like it is hard to tell whether she is an honest or good woman. The Wife like Giovanni is also eventually seen, through her desires, to fall into the grey zone. It's both the characters' desires and their pleasures that make them who they are, however Giovanni thinks his incestuous desires are not a kind of madness but making a comment on the society

---

9   Textual AO2 detail needed here, too. This is all very generalized.
10   An interesting claim which needs more attention.
11   An interesting, if a little untidy, exploration of motivation. The next two paragraphs provide some helpful AO2 substantiation.

he lives in, whereas the Wife of Bath just turns out to be stronger than her husbands in getting what she wants.[12]

If the characters in 'Tis Pity have moments of goodness, like the Friar and Cardinal, these turn out to be politically motivated, as everyone returns to arrogant and greed-filled ways. The Wife of Bath's story can be interpreted as a fantasy in which she gets what she wants after a life of disappointment, treating the Knight like a sexual fantasy, though it can also be interpreted as a feminist story as a metaphor for her own life and how she would like to end up.

Giovanni refuses to heed the way the Friar is shocked by his desires and in turn does achieve his wishes yet because he is in a revenge play his desires lead him to kill the woman he has wronged and he does not repent.[13]

The Wife continues to mock the Church and its teachings through her career as a Wife and her fate is unknown. However, when comparing her own life with the ugly lady in the tale we suspect she is not finished yet and will possibly take other lovers, even though her desires may bring her more 'tribulacion in mariage' if she marries a rapist like the Knight in her story.

Both Giovanni and the Wife are brought to madness by their own desires.[14] They have fallen into traps they themselves seem to be unable to pull themselves out of even if they wanted to. The Wife and the lovers seem to be so driven by their desires they've forgotten who they are and become caricatures of who they want to be. It's also strange how Giovanni, a man who during the Renaissance should be his own man, is only able to kill the person he loves in a bloody and brutal fashion. The Wife who lives in the Middle Ages when everything was supposed to be done by the book is so rebellious and is so much an individual at the mercy of her desires that we do not know if she is good or bad. Perhaps these characters' desires were not well suited to the worlds they lived in where sexual desire was often thought to drive people mad.

The strength of this answer lies in its vitality and allusiveness – the candidate has lots of ideas, and tends to operate by assertion, offering some AO2 justification later. The attempt to keep both texts constantly in play makes the essay feel rather disjointed: neither individual text gets quite the time or attention it seems to deserve. Nevertheless the answer does address the question and keeps it consistently in focus. Essentially informed and sound, this answer will probably gain a middle grade.

---

12 AO1 Handling both texts at once makes the argument rather indigestible, but a number of interesting points are raised here.
13 The AO3 comparison is only by implication, as the essay jumps from text to text. It's not always possible to see connections.
14 AO1 Reference back to the question.

Sample Essay Questions

1. 'The urge to control is in all of us: it drives our lives.'

In the light of this view, discuss ways in which writers represent the desire for control. In your answer, compare one drama text and one poetry text. **[30]**

2. 'Men embody lust: women exploit lust.'

In the light of this view, discuss the uses which writers make of sexuality. In your answer, compare one drama text and one poetry text. **[30]**

3. 'Through nature one finds peace.'

In the light of this view, consider the uses which writers make of the natural world. In your answer, compare one drama text and one poetry text. **[30]**

4. 'Deception is the spice of life.'

In the light of this view, consider ways in which writers explore deception. In your answer, compare one drama text and one poetry text. **[30]**

5. 'The wages of sin is death.'

In the light of this view, consider ways in which writers explore the sense of death. In your answer, compare one drama text and one poetry text. **[30]**

6. 'Mockery brings wisdom.'

In the light of this view, discuss ways in which writers make use of humour. In your answer, compare one drama text and one poetry text. **[30]**